# TRANSCIRCULARITIES

# TRANSCIRCULARITIES

*New and Selected Poems by Quincy Troupe*

COFFEE HOUSE PRESS

11/8/2002

To Burr

Poetry is the life-blood of literature, has helped me keep my sanity, heals and fuels my creative juices.

Hope you enjoy some of these,
all the best —

Quincy Troupe

COPYRIGHT © 2002 by Quincy Troupe
COVER ART © Edouard Duval Carrié (photographed by Kraig Cavanaugh)
AUTHOR PHOTOGRAPH by Lynda Koolish
BOOK DESIGN by Coffee House Press

The author extends his thanks to the editors of the following magazines, where some of these poems first appeared: *A Gathering of the Tribes, Another Chicago Magazine, Antioch Review, Black Creation, Black Renaissance Noire, Black Scholar, Black World,* BOPP, *Brilliant Corners, Callaloo, Chicago International, Code, Community Review, Confrontations, Conjunctions, Contact II, Crisis, Downtown Review, Drum, Drumvoices, Encore, Epoch, Essence, Eyeball, Filling Station, Hard Pressed, Helen Review, Indiana Review, Indigine, Iowa Review, Kenyon Review, Konch, Lapis, Long Shot, Lotus,* MARGIE: *The American Journal of Poetry, Miscellaneous Man, Mundus Artium, New Directions Annual, New York Quarterly, Nimrod, Nommo, Okike, Pequod, Ploughshares, Poetry Flash, Poets & Writers, Quilt, Review: Latin American Literature, River Styx, San Diego Monthly, See, Soul Illustrated, Sumac, Sunbury, The Best American Poetry 2000, The Mediterranean Review, The Village Voice, The Western Journal of Black Thought, The World, Tin House, Umbra, Vibrations, Vox, World Order, Yardbird,* and *Zyzzyva.*

Coffee House Press is a nonprofit literary publishing house. Support from private foundations, corporate giving programs, government programs, and generous individuals help make the publication of our books possible. We gratefully acknowledge their support in detail on the last page of this book.

Coffee House Press books are available to the trade through our primary distributor, Consortium Book Sales & Distribution, 1045 Westgate Drive, Saint Paul, MN 55114. For personal orders, catalogs, or other information, write to: Coffee House Press, 27 North Fourth Street, Suite 400, Minneapolis, MN 55401. Good books are brewing at www.coffeehousepress.org.

LIBRARY OF CONGRESS CIP INFORMATION
Troupe, Quincy.
    Transcircularities : new and selected poems / Quincy Troupe
        p. cm.
    ISBN 1-56689-135-3 (pbk. : alk. paper) — ISBN 1-56689-137-X (alk. paper)
        I. Title.

PS3570.R63 T73 2002
811'.54—DC21

2002081277

Except for minor alterations, the author and editors have decided to retain the stylistic choices, punctuation, and unique spellings of each book herein as they were originally published.

10  9  8  7  6  5  4  3  2  1
*first printing/first edition*

# CONTENTS

As always, to Margaret

and to Mother and the

memory of my Father

# I

EARLY POEMS, 1967–1969

## ODE TO JOHN COLTRANE

With soaring fingers of flame
you descended from Black Olympus
to blow about truth and pain: yeah,

just to tell a story about Black existence.
Then the flames left your fingers and soul,
came winter you lay down
in cold snow
and was cool.

But during bebop-filled avant-garde summers
you weaved slashing thunderclaps of sound
weaved spells of hypnotic beauty,
blew searing extensions of sublimation.

*Trane Trane runaway train smashing all known dimensions*
*Trane Trane runaway train smashing all known dimensions*

Hurtling thru spacelanes of jazz
a Black Phoenix of Third World redemption.

*eye say Trane Trane runaway train smashing all known dimensions*
*Trane Trane runaway train smashing all known dimensions*

With immortal pure sounds of brotherhood
turning and churning inside you,
boiling and steaming and exploding,
until reaching a stratified piety
whose deity was universal truth

*eye say Trane Trane runaway train smashing all known dimensions*
*Trane Trane runaway train smashing all known dimensions*

In sheets of sounds of injustice
you poured forth the bitter truth, the agony,
the pain, but making even that
seem beautiful too

*J.C. J.C. John Coltrane, J.C. J.C. John Coltrane*

You blew your fingers to smoking cinders
preparing for the "Ascension,"
blew beautiful sad death songs
on "Kind of Blue" mornings,
blew love on "A Love Supreme,"
now the ages await you,
beyond the infinite darkness
where the "Bird" of bebop slumbers.

But rage rage rage Coltrane!
Rage against the taking of a vision
Rage rage rage Coltrane!
Rage against the taking of Life!
For after Life eye know of no other vision.

And there is no guarantee
that one will follow bringing sight
to the place beyond my perception.

But eye concede to time/scarred myth of grand possibility.
eye concede to this, but to no more;
cause my life been filled with grand possibilities
but most have shut their doors.
But this be no mere cry of self/pity.
naw, eye don't look at life that way.

Eye am the pessimistic realist
who sees death as final and ugly;
waxed faces, unreal smells in mortuaries;
and flowers that rot upon mounded clay.

If Ojenke or Curtis Lyle were to die
eye would cry. Eye would remember times
that we ate and drank and laughed and chased
beauti/ful Black Women thru streets of Watts together.

Eye would remember new poetry
read in back rooms;
eloquent statements on the pig's inevitable doom:
bringing restoration of the waste of the people,
and that waste resurrected from the dance
upon smoking cinders of love.

Eye see death—as only eye can—
as a hushed kind of deep vast silence,
where roosters never crow
to herald the leaving of deadness,
where the clanking of chains is soundless
when dragged across the bottomless floor;
death is the infinite vigil beyond the door of Life:
death is the lengthening ocean of night
where there shines no light.

Yeah!—eye admit it!—death to me seems forbidding!
Descending into unexplored pits all alone;
pits of inescapable gloom where the air is heavy and dank,
where all flesh has fallen away leaving bones,
and soon the bones are no more,
only the crumbling grave/stone remains
to tell about who you were.

Death is weekends where great hornmen remain silent;
the "Bird" Lester Young Eric Dolphy Clifford Brown
except on ancient scratched-up records
on phonographs of old/timers
who lounge speaking of the good/old days
of dilapi/dated or polished rooms.

Those who followed you thru spring
thru summer thru autumn into winter,
those who watched you scatter the phalanx of jazz
and send them reeling and searching for cover,
those who remember your cry from "Round Midnight"
beauti/ful, esoteric, searing, when it flamed over
the entire sky, prelude to earth shaking thunder and fire
of "Equinox," these friends
who acknowledged your greatness quite early
will weep the hardest and the earliest.

Those who were familiar with your agony.
Those who were familiar with your pain.
Those who felt the hotness of manhood
surge like flames thru their veins, yeah!
these are the ones fear will not claim: they will cry;

*"Kulu Se Mama" "Kulu Se Mama" "Ole" "Ole" Coltrane!*
*"Kulu Se Mama" "Kulu Se Mama" "Ole" "Ole" Coltrane!*

Those who felt the prick of hypodermic death needles
hung off loaded in some shabby dark room,
who drinking wine and dying chased america's illusions
thru cold rank streets steeped in delusion
garbed in the evil mantle of white doom,

who sucked and fucked and jived and shucked
in strait-jacket tombs of insanity,
who came to the game in hopeless pain
and thought his mangled body to be the cobras fangs;
who died just to be doing something different.

Who were witch doctors of intrigue.
Who were voodoo/men of death.
Who were ghosts called hunger.
Who were men called sweat;
not men of "SEN-SEN" smelling death,
but men of halitosis smelling death!

{ *6* }

Who shot "smack" to ease the pain
of rapes by savages of innocent Black Mothers,
who shot "smack" to ease the torture
of lynchings by white savages
of noble Black Fathers,
who shot morphine to ease the agony
of "Blondes have more fun" type Black spinsters.
These ebony maidens who are prostitutes of the soul
who hoped and groped thru the "Jackie" mystique
went plunging and decadent into the "Twiggy" mystique;
lost Black beauti/ful Women: chasing images of impossibility

while dancin and swingin to the down blues beat
of the philosopher of the Black masses, yeah!
James Brown James Brown Black Brown James Brown!
splendid rhythm of hips that sway
sing you not a song for the Trane?
sing you not a tune of lamentation
for this sacred bard, this jujuman—like you
whose song was about pain and love
and whose heart was very gentle with love?

And you Johnny Mathis, nightingale with the clearest of chime,
will you not croon the Trane a line
of love and enduring admiration?

And what of you conceited weavers of rhyme?
You Poets, spilling unfinished drinks
upon the carpets of these times
sitting mesmerized by cheap wine
writing: "It's time it's time to write those lines
but I'm too drunk to do it now,
I'll wait until tomorrow to do it,
but it's time, it's time."

And tomorrow coming and going
leaving unquenchable footprints of yesterday,

and you the fearless warrior-poet
lying stone cold dead in your lead head
gripping an unfinished poem to Trane in your head.

Death has no sympathy for the unfinished.
And of genius and greatness? it feels
not one way or the other.
It simply comes like the exalted thing that it is:
alone, and unescorted into any room—this room perhaps!
bringing news of dimensionless wandering.

Yeah Trane! I'm gonna weep for you!
As will Miles blowing sad songs of style!
As will Poets writing wondrously sad elegies cry!

Yeah! I'm gonna weep for lost and pain Coltrane!
But during moments of future clarity
eye will see you as Black John the jujuman,
Black Phoenix who soared sky high! and even beyond!
breathing love fire light upon a dark vast night
speaking about years of monumental human agony!

Trane Trane John the Baptist, Ohnedaruth,
immortal burning flame of Black jazz,
jujuman running wild over galloping Black Music,
eye give to you this poem of remembrance,
the most sacred gift this poor Black man has.

Trane Trane John Coltrane, you came and while here
breathed light love upon cold red sky
dripping with blood death and fire
so that Black music love
would not falter and die,

eye say rest rest rest Coltrane
Trane Trane John Coltrane
and sleep the deep sleep
of all the ages. . . .

## POEM FOR FRIENDS

*for Calvin Hernton*

1.

the earth is a wonderful
yet morbid place
crisscrossing reaping complexities
of living

        seeking death
we go
with foot/steps
that are either heavy or light
(depending upon your weight

your substance)

go into light, or darkness
(depending upon the perception
of your vision)

we flounder, we climb
we trip
       we fall
         we call upon dead prophets
to help us
        yet

they do not answer

(we hear instead the singing in the leaves
the waves of oceans, pounding)

we see sheer cliffs
of mountains polished by storms
sculptured to god's perfection

we see the advancing age of technology
see soulless monsters

                eating up nature's perfections
hear wails & screams

             & sirens howling


but hear no human voices calling


we sit at the brink of chaos laughing
we idle away time
when there is no time
left us


we jump out of air/planes with no parachutes
we praise the foul mad/men of war
we are pygmalions

             in love with cold, bleak stones


& aphrodite is not here
          to save us
            seeking death


we come to origins
forks in the road of indecision
shaped like wishbones
& we go down unknown roads
seeking light in an ocean
of pure darkness


   2.
journey if you can
to the far poles of the world
there you will find flocks
of sick birds
dying in the blue sea that is sky
you will find herds of animals
huddled together in the snow

against the cold
with no feeling or touch
of each other, no knowledge
no love, dying in the fierce
blowtorching cold
yet they graze eagerly
into seas of light
meeting darkness


   3.
& the mind is so wide
& wide again
          so broad and deep
& deep, again
          far down we go so slow
to find knowledge
sad songs of who we are
but go slow from here
from everywhere, effendi
go slow into sadness
          of who we are
            where we are
go slow into slow dance of what
you are
        go slow into beauty
of space & time & distance
measure
        every breath that you breathe
for it is precious
       holy
          go free into sun/lit days
fly free like old african ibises
confronting the wind
swim long in the currents of these times
like the dolphin
        plunging through blue waves

for time is holy

& the faces that we see
upon the curl of the foam
               of the fingered blue waters
are the faces of the world, sandstones
falling through hourglasses
& deposited upon these shores
& they are seeds
in need of nourishment
in need of beauty, requesting wisdom
are children of the universe, glissando falling
upon these death-littered shores
that are reefs breaking rabid waves
seaweeds that remind of varicose veins
peeping up through the skin of these transparent
shallows—churning red waters beating up against
savage rocks, spiked with bones—
surrounding these islands
where all life buries itself
under rocks & sand

        4.
we must investigate our bodies
we must investigate our sources of beauty
we must investigate our exalted images
the parade of decayed heroes that we cheer
that we help invent
we must probe & descend into life/styles
like surgeons seeking cancer
we must cut away with truth's scalpel
all verbose flesh, all diseased portions
we must fly free & weightless
as a summer breeze
to nests in truth's sanctuary

5.

& the shell is bursting
from within
from without

& in order to go out
we must come in, again
so come in, come in, again
go out, go out, again
go out there now, effendi
          to the sweet places

where the good folks gather
              talk to everyone
for everyone is someone whose life is important to someone
to everyone
              whose flesh is a/part of your own

universe

so come in, come in, again
go out, go out, again

be beautiful for all people of the world

walk back into streets that are ours, effendi
walk back into hours & years carrying joy

go now, go now, go now
                    effendi
do your thang
do the righteous thang
for the world
for the world
to save the world
to save our children

to save yourself

# FOR MALCOLM, WHO WALKS
# IN THE EYES OF OUR CHILDREN

*for Porter, Solomon, Neruda & Assiatou*


he had been coming a very long time
had been here many times before
malcolm, in the flesh of other persons, malcolm
in the flesh of flying gods

his eyes had seen the flesh turned to stone
had seen stone turned to flesh
had swam within the minds of a billion great heroes
had walked among builders of nations
of the sphinx, had built with his own hands

those nations, had come flying across time
a cosmic spirit, a notion, an idea
a thought wave transcending flesh fusion of all
centuries, had come soaring like a sky break

above ominous clouds of sulfur, wearing
a wingspan so enormous it spanned the breath
of a people's bloodshed, had come singing

like coltrane, breathing life into miles
into stone-cold statues formed from earthworms & lies

malcolm, cosmic spirit who still walks back-straight
tall among us, here, in the words of nelson mandela
in the rap of public enemy number one, ourselves
deep down, we hear your lancing voice splitting wide open still
the pus-filled sores of self-hatred covering our bodies here
like scabs infested with AIDS—the poisoned
blood running out of us still stains the ground here, malcolm
creates bright red flowers of art everywhere—we stand up
our love for you & are counted in the open air—

hear your trumpet voice breaking here, like miles
zigzagging through the open prairie of our minds
in the form of a thunderbolt splitting the sky—& just before
your tornado words dip down inside an elephant trunk
conveying winds carrying the meaning of your words
shattering all notions of bullshit here—

we see your vision still in the life force of men & women
see you now in the high-flying confidence of our children, malcolm
who spread their enormous wingspans & fly through their minds
with confidence, mirroring the beauty you stood for, brother—

your spirit, malcolm, burning in the suns of their eyes

# 2

---

FROM EMBRYO, 1971

## COME SING A SONG

Come sing a song, Black Man,
sing of Blind Joe Death,
sing a blues,
sing a black-blues song,
sing a Blind Joe Death blues song,
sing a work song,
sing a prison chain gang
southern blues worksong,
sing jazz, rock, or, R & B,
sing a song Black Man,
sing a "bad" freedom song

## SOUTH AFRICAN BLOODSTONE
*for Hugh Masekela*


South African bloodstone
drenched with the soil
drenched with the beauty
of the drum-drum beat of land

drenched with the beauty
of God's first creation of man

& sculpted into lean hawk look
eyes burning deep
                        bold diamonds of fire
dance sing music to the air

Conjureman/conjure up
the rhythm of voodoo walk
weave the spell/paint the trance
began the fire ritual

Hugh Masekela! homeboy
from the original home/going home
play your horn your trumpet horn
screech scream speak of ancestors

Conjureman/conjure up
the memory of ancestral lands
the easy walk the rhythmic walk
click click talk of trumpet genius

Hugh Masekela homeboy
from the original home going home

Speak South African bloodstone speak!

# PROFILIN, A RAP/POEM
*for Leon Damas*


People be profilin.

People be profilin like
stink on shit,
like come/sweat for money,
like toe-jam doodoo smell

barbecue-wine stains
on picnics in july,
people be profilin everyday
                              of their lives

People be profilin.

People be profilin like
slick stylin pimps leanin bent
at forty-five degree angles
behind mink covered steerin wheels
of cold-gold lamed el dorados
with golden brown velvet roofs for tops
wide brimmed apple hats
pulled rakishly down
slashes their scowling mugs

(& the sun dont melt
the "ice" these frozen nigga
mackmen wear
on their manicured fingers!)

People be profilin.
People be profilin everyday
                              of their lives

{ *21* }

People be profilin.

People be profilin like
whores on midtown Manhattan streets corners,
like Wall Street executives in their sterile
                              looking
dark, conservative suits,
their brains wrapped in green mothballs,
like bigtime "Media" intellectuals
styled off
behind their gold wire rimmed
expensive clear lens-shades

People be profilin.
People be profilin everyday
                    of their lives

People be profilin.
People be profilin like
sad media stars who say;
"Oh no dear! dont take that
side of my face,
its bad for my public image!"

(& can you dig where that
whole thing is coming from?!)

People be profilin.
People be profilin like
when you stick a camera
into someone's face,
be they Kings, or Queens,
or the President of these United Snakes,
watch how they react to the camera!

(unless they be too old, or too tired,
or too dead for this daily crazy shit)

People be profilin.
People be profilin everyday
                    of their lives

People be profilin.

## MIDTOWN TRAFFIC

Black jazz piano
struttin' across
Central Park,
flowing from hidden
Park Avenue radios

& further down
cars jammed down
into mid-town traffic
musicians layin down their
own original tunes of

*toot toot & honk loud horns*

Between dissonance of being
screamed on by plenty ugly
lookin cursin cold
purple red bastards
pushin
beat-up
growlin trucks,
beetle-sized,
hog-sized

dartin slashin
faintin wise

dented
schemin
cars movin through

new york claw of traffic
crowded with the lives
of beautiful stylin ladies

{ 24 }

odd schizoids,
people that talk
to themselves constantly
longside nose runnin
junkies doin a
grotesque sag dance
in search of a scratch
for an itch

Fast movin traffic
of black jazz piano
high, creating blues,

anchored breezes
filled with cocaine

& rock guitars.

CHICAGO
*for Howlin Wolf*


I.

The wind/blade cutting in
& out swinging in over the lake
slicing white foam from the tips
of delicate water fingers
that danced & weaved
under the sunken light/night;
this wind/blade was so sharp & cold
it'd cut a four-legged mosquito into fours
while a hungry lion slept on the wings of some chittlins
slept within the blues of a poem that was formin

We came in the sulphuric night drinkin old crow
while a blizzard licked its beak atop the head of tricky nixon
while gluttonous daley ate hundreds of pigs that were his ego
while daddy-o played bop on the box
came to the bituminous breath of chicago
howling with three-million voices of pain

& this is the music;
the kids of chicago have eyes that are older
                              than the deepest pain in the world
& they run with bare feet over south/side streets
shimmering with shivers of glass
razors that never seem to cut their feet;
they dance in & out of traffic—
the friday night smells of fish
& hog maws, the scoobedoo
sounds of bo diddley

{ *26* }

2.

These streets belong to the dues/payer
to the blues/player/drinking whiskey on satadaynight
muddy waters & the wolfman howlin     smokestack lightnin
how many more years     down in the bottom
no place to go   moanin for my baby
a spoonful     of evil
back door man
all night long     how many more years
down in the bottom   built for comfort

## THE SYNTAX OF THE MIND GRIPS

the syntax of the mind grips
the geography of letters
the symbol burns, leaves, black
ocean bleeds pearls/washing the shore
darkness crawls in alone like a panther
all luminous eyes watching us make
love, under trees the beautiful
woman in the grass curls
her pulling legs
around my shoulders
the old maid weeps in the window
covers her face with blue veined white hands,
her fingernails painted red
gouges out her love-shattered eyes
while the mirror breaks in the bathroom
falls like razors to the floor
where a junkie is sprawled
with a death needle in his arm
a child cuts his feet in the streets
screams for the old maid
who makes the flags
who is weeping in the window
because the stars have fallen from the flags
she does not hear anything
but her own weeping
hanging, the flag has become a garrote
choking the breath/love of a people
whose hero is the armless/legless brainless
vegetable who sits upon his bandaged stump
in a wheel/chair, in a veteran's
hospital in washington;
he cannot speak-tell the blood
he has swallowed;
he cannot see for the death

his eyes have seen;
he cannot hear for the screams
his ears have heard; but he feels
the sorrow of the old maid
who is weeping because the stars
have fallen from the flag
and because of the love scene
in wet grass beneath her window

# WEATHER REPORT IN
# LINCOLN NEBRASKA 2/8/71
*"It is the coldest night in 23 years in Lincoln Nebraska"*


Outside my see-through mirror
snow was piled in frozen sculpture
grotesque along the bleak streets
of Lincoln Nebraska
while on television Apollo 14
streaked through unconquered space
after photographing holes
and collecting weird rocks on a moon
that did not welcome them, also on this day
america was invading Laos disguised as
south vietnamese troops; (they recruited
a lot of slant eyed american dwarfs and hired
america's best makeup men to pull off
this standard american hat-trick.)

And in Lincoln Nebraska the temperature
was twenty-three degrees below zero
but it was colder than that
within the pentagoned ruled executive tombs
in washington; it was so cold that nobody
as yet has recorded the temperature,
and this suited
richie just fine
as he walked around naked
took a sauna bath in a tub
filled with Laotian blood while his
handmade good-old melvin scrubbed
his brain clean with a redwhiteand blue
soapbar of pure nitroglycerin

## WHITE WEEKEND
*April 5–8, 1968*


They deployed military troops
surrounded the White House
and on the steps of the Senate building
a soldier behind a machine gun

32,000 in Washington & Chicago
1900 in Baltimore Maryland
76 cities in flames on the landscape
and the bearer of peace
lying still in Atlanta

Lamentations! Lamentations! Lamentations!
Worldwide!
But in New York, on Wall Street,
the stock market went up 18 points . . .

## WOKE UP CRYING THE BLUES

Woke up crying the blues:
bore witness to the sadness of the day;
the peaceful man from Atlanta
was slaughtered yester/day.
Got myself together
drank in the sweetness of sun/shine,
wrote three poems to the peace/ful lamb
from Atlanta; made love
to a raging Black woman
drank wine
got high: saw angels
leading the lamb to heaven?
the blues gonna get me
gonna get me for sure!
went to the beach/to forget
if only eye can
about th gentle soul from Georgia;
ate clam chowder soup and fish sandwiches;
made love in the sand
to this same beautiful woman
drank in all her sweetness:
lost future child in the sand,
saw the bloody sun falling
behind  weeping purple clouds;
tears fell in rivers for this gentle lamb
who eye can't forget.
The bloody star sinking
into the purple grave: blackness falls.
Go out into the decay of day;
copped three keys;
*the key of happiness,*
*the key of creative joy,*
*the key of sadness.*
Came back, watched the gloom on the tube

at her house; which was disrupted.
Kissed her, went home by the route
of the mad space ways: dropped tears in my lap
for the lamb from Atlanta.
Home at last.
Two letters under the door;
a love letter from the past
grips at the roots of memory
at last another poem published!
good news during a bad news' weekend;
lights out;
drink of grapes;
severed sight closes
another day
in the life.

VISION


Dreaming
eye went into razor/edged streets
& thought Watts to be beautiful that day

Children danced freely
in fervor of their energy
the laser eye baked joy into their songs
sisters FINE AS COLD DUCK BURGUNDY
swung their TO COLD BLACK ASSES
under the hung sun   gave out
passionate kisses
yeah!
& brothers
beating conga drums in parks
traded stale pale men
back for dark rum

massacred
the antique people of suburbia
the super freak draculas of babylon

Brothers smashed
the concrete heads of political snakes
tricky dick & mickey mouse found
dead in comic strips
& dick tracy didnt give a damn
which was the trick
as long as he got
his front
money

Eye heard jimmy smith cookin
like a geee eeeeeeeee electric range

burnin homemade mash potatoes
chicken & dumplins
with fried cakes
& greens on the side

Eye heard laughter spilling over empty plates
slick from lickings of hungry tongues
saw popes & bishops sprinkling
holy water
& giving blessings
to atomic bombs
postmarked for china

& can you believe
eye saw a chinese church of the nazarene that day
where coolies steeped in dream horror fantasy of america
nailed their hands to the wall & drove spikes
of assimilation deep into their brains,
& then eye heard *eric dolphy* began to cry
from the depths of whatever pained him
heard him play a funereal bar of parting

watched him climb the creaking stairs of bebop
watched him enter *tranes* room with a smile
& sit down to play the *new music*
far removed from our straining eyes

& then eye woke up to the howl of wolves baying,
whiskey glasses empty on the table,
heard the deep deep snore
of black friends drunk
on the couch of capitalism,
saw the deathgun
staring in my face;
& then eye prayed, & then eye cried;

"Allah, O Merciful One, dont let the fires
   of the devil take my soul & song"

& then came a flash

& then was the last thing

eye saw

or heard.

# IN TEXAS GRASS

all along the rail
road tracks of texas
old train cars lay
rusted & overturned
like new african governments
long forgotten by the people
who built & rode them
till they couldnt run no more,
they remind me of old race horses
who've been put out to pasture
amongst the weeds
rain sleet & snow
till they die, rot away,
like photos fading
in grandma's picture book,
of old black men in mississippi/texas
who sit on dilapidated porches,
that fall away
like dead man's skin,
like white people's eyes,
& on the peeling photos,
old men sit sad-eyed
waiting, waiting for
worm dust, thinking of
the master & his long forgotten
promise of 40 acres & a mule,
& even now, if you pass across
this bleeding flesh
changing landscape,
you will see fruited
countryside, stretching, stretching,
old black men, & young black men,
sittin on porches
waiting, waiting for rusted
trains in texas grass

# THREE FOR THE BIAFRAN WAR

1.
the wet eye
of a woman
in love is both
beauti/ful
glorious
& sad

2.
a man
is the sun
of his son
& rain most
time falls
where it's
the warmest

3.
a child
is the voice
closest to
the past
& the ancestors
who are pure
African spirits
& love
everyone
& every
thing

## IN SEVENTY-FIVE SYLLABLES

We are here in this space place,
as life is locked to air,

welding seeds of our singing,
as black day weds the night,

moon plays infinite rituals,
as gold clouds devour the stars

black minotaurs bleed the blues,
eat eggs white with eclipse,

where music fucks the easel
pure rhythm paints the day

in seventy-five syllables

# IN THE MANNER OF RABEARIVELLO*

On sea without motion
a man holding a thousand skies
on his black head that has no color
a man on the blue flame of suicides
finger tips & glides/turns/yearns
always to be more
than simple man with anchored thighs

Night comes with its leopardhide like counterpoint
wraps around today's wingless promise shipwrecked
at the bottom of scooped out oceans

& the day vomits out without music
where blood drips up from the sky/eye
the earth disappears beyond the edges

& at the bottom of white volcanos 1000 sharks
struggle to swim free of the grip
of a hundred boneless skeletons
while at high/noon
amongst invisible tree/poems in madagascar
rabearivello hovers amongst the branches
& sings his mournful dirge of mystery

while children crawl out without legs
towards a sea that has no motion
that is washed red by the ink
of the sky
that is filled by a poet's
eye always capsizing

Jean-Joseph Rabearivello (1901-1937) was one of the most remarkable poets of this century. A Madagascarian poet, he
was completely original in the last half of his life. He always seemed to write in a dream-like trance, conjuring up
remarkable cosmic images, totally contradictory, impossible to believe images. He has been called a pure African/
surreal poet. He wrote in French. He died, a suicide in 1937, in Madagascar.

# DREAM POEM/SONG

silence, silence on the roads
blending with wind/song
that is also silent,
silent are words though spoken
with microphones amplified through anger,
with flames, silent the sound of four-
string guitars played by sightless donkeys
in the road, in the middle of the road
blind donkeys sit playing
silent four-string guitars,

& silent are the stampeding herds
of butchered headless elephants,
silent the bear trapped raging
in steel-fanged trappers grip,
though the blood gushes out washing the pear
fallen from branches, the earth beneath
receives no storm released blood/drops
that are tears for a grave
of darkness no longer hearing music,

not even natures woodwinds/Coltrane
amongst branches singing love
drowned out by lynch mobs,

though the blood gushes out washing the pear
though the blood gushes out staining the pear

in the streets where an empty junk wagon
with rickety wheels of hunger
rattles soundlessly over cobblestone bricks

the blood stains the wheels stains the pear
bleeding over bells pleading of plunder

soundless the squeals of cancerous hunger
silent the clamorous voices of bloating corpses
of sinsane voices, silent the proclamations,
theories, revolutionary slogans
numerous as revolutionary buttons
replacing substance with rattling voices
of silence, the total noise of absurdity
of hatred-filling the air with their silence,

silence on the roads filled with blood & corpses
silence blending with wind/song, wheeling
across centuries that are also silent
bleeding silences within silences
breeding silences within silences

though the blood gushes out staining the pear
in the road, in the middle of the road
blind donkeys sit playing
silent four-string guitars,
& silent the stampeding herds of butchered
headless elephants, silent the rage of the bear

RAIN/TIME

In a hurricane of dust morning
this man jumped sideways out of a dream
dressed in black,
jumped right out of his own bleeding thumb,
and standing wide-legged in the middle
of the bone road,
in the middle of a corpse crowded road,
drew a gun that shot out fast
from a fast drooping barrel of flesh,
that reminded me of an old military man's penis
after this daily hetacombs,
and after everytime he thinks about
sex, shot out
from the eye of that drooping black barrel,
sleeping gristle,
where the moon crawls into hide
everytime the sun bursts spitting down
its lasered sword/shaft of death,
on the deserts at high noon in the fire-time,
shot-out into cloud of bleached bone
fang-night
slashing rain-time,
in needle rain-time,
a song-decree slithering
from fast-drooping black barrel

transformed into hurricane
of dust morning
like a wild-eyed cobra trying to escape
from a red-eyed purple mongoose,
who leaped out from yellow cough
of limping smoke
weeping from the eye
of that invisible cold barrel,

leaped out into rain-time,
dressed in black,
serious as a final heart-attack,
serious, dead serious as cancer.

## DREAM/DANCE

seven wingless syllables dance
peal across blues of chanting rivers
swim within cathedrals grown from bones
huckabuck across electric circus tables
synchronized to unchanging faces of stone
fourteen perfect anachronisms
creep within the bleeding dome of the soul
plunge towards the black/dead face of the sun
eclipsed by a solo of the Bird
eleven soundless syllables wrapped in stone
& dead from overliving chant of silence
weeping red tears within the temperate zone
between silence oblivious death
thirteen perfect breaths cylindrically
symmetrical hang from fifty bleeding
money trees in washington
& thirteen perfect deaths dance in stone
unknown/thirteen soundless syllables
wrapped in stone   dream/dance

## BIRDS FLY WITHOUT MOTION
## TO THE SUMMIT


when the air freezes into heat
birds fly without motion to the summit

where the flag of despair is planted
death rushes headlong into the blood
and time rolls like a tide backwards

the hours run slipping on banana peels
and the skeletons rattle night-seeking flesh
where the dead masquerade as the living

the eyes seek heights of the sightless

where birds fly without motion to the summit
the air dressed like a clown freezes into night

## BENEATH THE BLUEST SEA

Birds flap crumbling wings
beneath tailfire of metal hawks.

Distance deepens
as the last deep breath
of the fish-man swimming within the falling
dark void
slips away; as

flesh falls away from
bone, as time drops blood
into inkwells
death filled with piranhas & sharks.

All around,
the earth grows cities
upon mountainous sinking brow of edges.

Here,
people sink into themselves;
within hours/steps,
flesh hangs loose from bones.

# EMBRYO

1.
We come from earth
mother give us your blood
give us strong love to become

seed of water-spirit
sunbird of love in flight

poetry of birth in motion

strength of cyclic movement
in a family of plane curves

locus of points that move
the ratio
distance of fixed point
to distance
of fixed line

poetry of birth in motion

that is infinite
plane curve formed
in the water-spirit womb

of the axis
the intersected cone
locus of points summing

sunbird of love birth in flight

distances fixing constants
wind/storm   rain   air   water
sun   earth   spirit-birth

point of departure
found in beginnings that ripen

germinating embryo
sprung African shades of ancestors
flung from petals of flowers into
bloodstreams of harvesting eyewinds

poetry of birth in motion

& carried to distant planes
that sing not from wombseeds
of Georgia Tennessee & Missouri
where life sometimes begins & ends

in wombs of concrete labyrinths

2.

Life is molten rocks
spilling out from lips of volcanos
red/orange finger rivers
that destroy to give birth
within wombs of solid black rock

seed of water-spirit
sunbird of love in flight

poetry of birth in motion

fire songs of snake twisting motion
slide glide stride of hip dipping motion

sunbird of birth in flight

raising flame prayers to sun gods

offering up sacrifices of trees
animals   reptiles   insects   villages

seeds of water-spirit

sunbird of flames in flight

burning from guitar strings
of Jimi Hendrix    climbing from
saxophone bell of Ohnedaruth
mystical birds high in the water-spirit night

& in hot pitch-dark a black cat
carrying two suns in the eclipse of his head
swallows two fireflies climbing eyes
in the cavern of night

& the fire-ball that is swallowed
by the Pacific Ocean each sunken dusk
& who burns through earth spirit-water

leaps now from tips of devastated cities
leaps now from delicate Chinese finger paintings
leaps now from spitting barrels to coughing volcanos

leaps now into sunbird of birth in flight

& burns like a one-eyed black cat eclipsed
in hotpitch-dark    in hotpitch-dark
climbs a firefly born in the night

poetry of birth in motion

sunbird of love in flight

seed of water-spirit

## 3

FROM SNAKE-BACK SOLOS, 1979

## ASH DOORS & JUJU GUITARS

we have come through doors flaming
ashes the sad written legacy
smoldering bones heaped in pyres behind us

& yet campfire blues people singing
softly still under blue black moonlight

ash doors & juju guitars conjurin ancestral flights

sweet memories of shaman juju men
cotton-eyed bands croonin
softly the guitar-woman stroked enjoins

blues chanting mantras across throbbing land

at the flight of sun     light
at the flight of sun     light

## UP SUN SOUTH OF ALASKA:
## A SHORT AFRICAN AMERICAN HISTORY SONG

*for my son, Brandon Troupe*


1.

slit balls hung in southern/american winds then
when drumheads were slit made mum by rum
& songs hung way down
around our ankles bleeding up sun south of alaska
swinging silhouettes picked clean to bone
by black crows
caw caw razor scars black-winged crows ripping
sunset flights of slashing razors
crows crows
blues caw caws & moans
& blues caw caws & moans

then sunsets dangled voices
crowing blues caw caws black crowing razors streak
silhouettes against a frying skillet sky
broken necks & sun-gored bodies blistered in eclipse
hung nails rope burned
into sweet black lives

rip of pendulum razors
lays open the quaking earth of flesh/moans
from blue-black dues paying women
dropping embryos into quicksand
african secret songs strapped across blood-stained blades
of glittering american razors
songs of sun/down flesh karintha dusk flesh
drug through spit/ripped
bleeding up sun south of alaska
bleeding up sun south of alaska

2.

& crows & razors & ropes & bullets
crows & razors & ropes & bullets
the shared cold legacy
& crazed pale men lassoing the sun out of the sky
& darkness then bleeding up sun south of alaska
crow wings covering the sky & our eyes & their eyes too
eclipsing the face of the sun
now an invisible clock with laser-beamed hands
that are branding rays burning our flesh
reduced over time to bone/dust
kissing stone but the nature of stone
is not moved by the tongue of heat entering
the mouth of our lives—passionate sweet touch of meaning

but still we move through space towards grace
carrying a sphinx in one eye
a guitar in the other knowing that time is always
in the possession of the keeper


3.

so now son black
roll the pages of your american eyes back son
black son roll them back black son american
son way way back son
back before the sun ripped your flesh here
way way back sun
for the pages of your eyes carry the memory son
they are blue-black pages dues pages fingers strumming
music of oral history songs griot songs
african songs
strong black strumming fingers son
american black lives as humming caw caws

black crows transformed into eagles

no matter ripping suns son
no matter slit drums/tongues
we are here son
are sun music spirit son
caw caw blues razors

keepers of secret guitars

## THESE CROSSINGS, THESE WORDS
*for Pablo Neruda*

where will they take us to
these crossings
over rivers of blood-stained words
syllables haphazardly thrown together
as marriages that fall apart
in one day

we have come this far in space
to know nothing of time
of the imprisoning distance travelled
the scab-fleshed hobos passed
we have most times asked nothing

of the mirrors of our own shattered reflections
passing us as lava smoldering in the streets

in our red eyes the guillotine
smile of the hangman
a time-bomb ticking for our hearts
the brain an item bought like so much gooey candy
the laugh a razor's flash
the party time juba
of My Lai's sickening ritual

as american as elvis presley's dead days

& the blood-scarred wind
whipped rag blue squared off with starts
that are silver bullets
& pin-striped with bones of mythologized peppermint
will not hide the corpse-lynched history
hanging there twisting slowly
as a black man's body

screaming through soft magnolia air
over a tear-stained bride's veil
breeze blown & fluttering
as a flopping fish
in a gesture of surrender

we have come all this distance in darkness
bomb-flashes guiding our way
speaking of love/of passions instantly eclipsed
to find this corpse of freedom hung & machine-gunned
for the blood of a name beneath a simple word
(& what do we know who have not gone there in truth
of the roots of these flames burning at river-crossings
of the crossbones of our names connecting rivers
of blood beautiful as a fusing coltrane solo?)

& there are times when we see
celluloid phantoms of mediarized lovers
crawling from sockets of cracking up skeletons
posing as cameras & t.v. screens

times still when we stand here
anchored to silence by terror
of our own voice & of the face revealed
in the unclean mirror shattering
our sad-faced children
dragging anchors of this gluttonous
debauchery & of this madness
that continues to last

SNAKE-SONG SLITHERING
TOWARDS EVEL
*for Evel Knievel*

> *"The United States has not lost a past,*
> *it has lost its future."*
> —OCTAVIO PAZ

it is the last bells tolling
of twelve o'clock midnight
of the last year
during the last moments
of disaster/snake eyes

       disaster/snake eyes

deuce game
of snake twins
(eyes locked broken
between parentheses).

       in dual deaths
       of loaded crap games

two bones over
graveyard green rolling
as in a golf game bold cold toll of snakes
black spots
on paper thin ash white skulls

       beyond death
        beyond polished bones

snake cold    snake bold

twist double/time steel
snaking worm moles through dark twelve o'clock
stark midnight pits of tunneled hours     drag
of final years
fearing the final moment

        of disaster/snake cross

            snake toll

& O the ego strikes cold
bold snakebites
between parentheses

        between disasters

snake dark
snakepits bleached white
staked skeletons on sand under sun
millions of ants swarm
from scarfed-out eye sockets
run screaming everywhere
question marks of rib cages
fossilized american bones
everywhere sun bleached

        silence everywhere

bones run under scorching sun
alongside snakes slithering creating patterns
on sand belly down zig-zag runs on sand
creating crucifixes of language
as the faith is eaten clean

        as wormed flesh of George

Washington/bridge
falling down   watergate(s) flooded
cities gored by their own ignorance
as voices of bleached rib cages speak
wind-sand saws through bones
frictioned clean
by piranha teeth violence
of time's sad language

      of mad wars laid bare

rattlesnakes amongst the vertebrae
boned terror as silence grips polluted air
hulls of sunken ships
wing spans of crashed airplanes
museum space skeletons of Cape Kennedy
corporate garbage peaks of power dreams
masticated voices
sunken ruins of shrivelled flesh
skulls as bobbing cigarette butts
in stagnant unused coffee cups
pythons of greed crushing
life breath returned to death

snake cold   snake bold
& O sad ego strike bold
cold snakebites
between parentheses

      between disasters

cobra-blooded
fanging frozen people

it's so coldly muddled
America/dreaming & screaming
it's so cold-blooded

America now

# NEW YORK CITY BEGGAR

his body held the continence
of a protruding tongue
of a hanged man twisting & turning
in sweltering needle-sharp heat
held the continence
of a jet plane's high propulsion saliva
his body swollen as a toilet stool
packed full of a two-day-old shit
warts crawling like frenzied roaches
over his skin of yellow fever
bloated as the graves of earth
or jammed as rivers full
of lynched black bodies—
sores popping open through ventilated
clothing like hungry termites
devouring flesh
the texture of quivering pus

& he looked at me
with the look of a wrung-necked chicken
with that of a somnambulist
blasted by poison of thunderbird wine
storms his eyes streaked red
with crow-wings raking corners
of his peppermint moons
like claws of a rooster

& his fingernails   the color of tadpoles
sought the origin of a 400-year-old itch
which held the history
& secret of crushed indian bones
& of clamoring moaning voices
of unborn black children who were
screaming semen of castrated nigga dicks

& his look held the origin of ashes
the blood-stained legacy of sawdust on the floor
of a butcher
                     & his rasping sawblade voice cutting
held the unmistakable calligraphy of lepers
who with elephantiasis feet drag themselves across
sword blades of murderous pentagon juntas

(which is the history of reared-back cobra snakes
which is the truth of the game we're in.)

& when he spoke to me
his maggot-swarming words reeking of outhouses
"brother, can you spare a dime?"
his spirit low as coaldust
his energy drained as transparent shells
of sunstricken cockroaches his breath
smelling of rotten fish markets
his teeth looking like chipped tombstones
nicked away in a hurricane of razors
eye heard a forked-tongue capitalist
on wall street fart & croak

(which is the history of reared-back king cobras
which is the truth of the game we're in.)

& when eye walked away with my dime
still chattering in my pocket
he put a halloween leer on me said "thank you,
boss" gave the V for victory/peace sign
cursed under his breath
& left like an apparition flapping
his raggedy black coat
like giant crow wings in the wind

## AFTER HEARING A RADIO ANNOUNCEMENT:
## A COMMENT ON SOME CONDITIONS

yesterday in new york city
the gravediggers went on strike
& today the undertakers went on strike
because they said of the overwhelming
amount of corpses
(unnecessarily they said because
of wars & stupid killings in the streets
& etcetera & etcetera.)

sweating the world     corpses
propped up straight in living room chairs
clogging up rivers     jamming up freeways
stopping up elevators     in the gutters     corpses
everywhere you turn
& the undertakers said that they were
being overworked with all this goddamned killing
going on     said that they couldn't even enjoy
all the money they was making
said that this shit has got to stop

& today eye just heard that
the coffin-makers are waiting in the wings
for their chance to do the same thing
& tomorrow & if things keep going this way
eye expect to hear of the corpses
themselves boycotting death
until things get better
or at least getting themselves
together in sort of union-espousing
self-determination
for better funeral &
burial conditions
or something extraordinarily
heavy like that

## STEEL POLES GIVE BACK NO SWEAT
*after Waring Cuney*


in new york city people
cop their own posts
underground waiting on subway platforms
lean up against them
claim them as their own
ground & space

while up over ground
winds scrape the back of skies piercing
poles of concrete laced with laughing quicksilver
mirrors square phallic symbols
in their glint
of limp-dick capitalism
repositories for fallen
pigeon shit

below them stoned bums
scrape their lives into asphalt sleep
on sidewalks slow shuffle scabby bruised feet towards terrors
only they know
leaning underground
against graffitied steel subway poles
alone carrying their feverish frenzy
that needed bathing long ago

& so each day here we pass
each other waiting for love to speak
to us to everyone so slow in coming here
to cleanse our needs of these terrible wounds
scraped raw by these clawing days
leaning forward into one another
our lives touching here
these underground steel poles

propping up our bodies
flawed by breath
& anointed with scents
from wherever it is we are coming from

& can feel the flesh rubbing steel
& think the steel flesh
& tell ourselves we are not lonely here
couldn't be lonely
here in this gargantuan city
where steel poles
give back no sweat

SNOW & ICE

ice sheets sweep this slick mirrored darkness
as keys that turn tight trigger brains
of situations
where we move ever so slowly
            so gently into time-spaced agony
bright turning of imagination
so slowly
through revolving doors opening up to enter mountains
where spirits walk voices so slowly swept
by cold breathing fire
            as these elliptical moments of illusion
fragile loves sunk deep in snows as footprints
weak chained black gesticulations
bone bared voices
            chewed skeletal choices
in fangs of vampirish gales
these silver slivers of raucous laughter
glinting bright as hard polished nails

# A SURREALISTIC POEM TO EVERYONE
# & NO ONE IN PARTICULAR


high above the ceiling of imagination
crescendo thunderclaps of silence
before lightning a tongue of pearls slashing
the tapestry of God's eye
totemic gongringer of cocaine spells
consummate tapdancer on the holy rings
around saturn
        hydraulic wingbeater
of a dehydrated eagle
laid back soothsayer
who sees the world as one grain of sand
cosmic mindsmoker of the seven skies of dewdrops & doowops
righteous deep sea diver
of the hot sucking womb

this tomb-headed chronicler of the dark
secrets of the vatican
omnipotent court jester
        of the kingdom of novocaine
stomp down choreographer of nod & stumble
junkie ballets
scientific finder of collapsed river veins
molecular rhesus monkey of the ultimate trip of battery acid
peyote sky tripper eater of jagged sharp tin cans
fire swallowing termite of esoteric books
bringer of hot-ice seasons of unknown climates
gri-gri stone eater of broken lightbulbs
bubonic trigger man of no hesitation

out here your test-tube children wearing
uniforms full of worthless medals wearing tight-fitting suits
with buttons popping club-footed dancers
of wet dream midnights

totemic gongringer of cocaine spells
all these desert-fried faces
of sandstorms/chopped iguanas
rattlesnaking eyeballs swarming with garbage
flies sweating speech as buzzsaws of termites
cutting through redwood trees
night-trippers of onion & garlic kisses
toe-tappers of naked nose rubbing eskimos
bellringers of sandpaper pussies
sardine flesh rappers of cat-shit breath

whose eyes gleam sharp as piranha teeth
whose skunk smelling sword blade words reek
of no consequence & nixonian intentions blubberous
jellyfishes of short legs knobby knees
& long flat-footed premonitions

no doubt about it gongringer
the brain of mankind is sometimes a piss
of swiss cheese on the plate of a beggar

## FROM RICHMOND COLLEGE,
## POSTMARKED——MANHATTAN

from this plate-glass window
high above staten island
night closes in on the jugular vein of day
as black paint spreads down over space
of white canvas
squeezing out the life
cycle of day

artificial lights shimmer/dance
bojangle out of focus
tap-dance across the sound stuffed with slow moving ships
as the verrazano bridge strings out its chainlink
of stars/glittering notions
blurs of flashing carlights
rippling motions

& from here across the sound's
waters the shore of brooklyn comes alive with yellow
lights that glow
like eyes of panthers

headlights shutter/blink
down freeways carved from blood & stolen gold
while the american flag shivers/whips back
hung up there atop staten island's
city hall tower
alone in the face of ice
cold winds
black hands on the white face
of the luminous tower clock
move methodically

while under the bridge
the strung-out motion red
lights pulsate like heartbeats
of a rebreathing bag/dreams
rise & fall against the darkness
blood colors
bloodshot eyes in flight
feverish eyes of countless rodents
impressionistic images swirling
penetrate the dark rhythms

while down at the ferry landing
cars move like monstrous bugs
down long curving rampways
headlight tongues for eyes probe/open up
the darkness with their bone bright keys of light
crawl up the snaking asphalt pavement
while people move in slow
fast shuffling motion as in old homemade
silent movies in black & white dragging
their day behind them
anchored to tired drooping shoulders

now across the sound
in the other direction towards manhattan
the eye locates the oxidized green french
woman carved from stone lighting her torch
in the harbor
while manhattan looms up behind her
a gigantic electric circus
of sizzling lights

now light closes in finally
its walls of mystery like dracula
enfolding himself up in his black sweeping cape
while all around staten island supper smells
tantalize the nostrils

now as eye am leaving
the wind dies
down up on the flagpole the flag hangs limply
while black hands on the white face of the clock
turn around the hours fast as jessie owens
winning the olympic dashes
in hitler's germany in 1936

now panther against the dark
eye enter the ferry
slip down through the womb of its doors
like a letter being slid into
an envelope

slides back into the night
postmarked; manhattan

# THE OLD PEOPLE SPEAK OF DEATH

*for Leona Smith, my grandmother*

the old people speak of death
frequently now
my grandmother speaks of those now
gone to spirit
now less than bone

they speak of shadows
that graced their days made lovelier
by their wings of light speak of years
& corpses of years of darkness
& of relationships buried
deeper even than residue of bone
gone now beyond hardness
gone now beyond form

they smile now from ingrown roots
of beginnings of those who have left us
& climbed back through the holes the old folks
left in their eyes
for them to enter through

eye walk back now with this poem
through the holes the old folks left in their eyes
for me to enter through walk back to where
eye see them there
the ones that have gone beyond hardness
the ones that have gone beyond form
see them there
darker than where roots began
& lighter than where they go
with their spirits
heavier than stone their memories
sometimes brighter than the flash

of sudden lightning
but green branches will grow
from these roots darker than time
& blacker than even the ashes of nations
sweet flowers will sprout
& wave their love-stroked language
in sun-tongued morning's shadow
the spirit in all our eyes

they have gone now back
to shadow as eye climb back out
from the holes of these old folks eyes
those spirits who sing through this poem
gone now back with their spirits
to fuse with greenness
enter stones & glue their invisible
faces upon the transmigration of earth
nailing winds singing guitar blues
voices through ribcages
of these days
gone now to where the years run
darker than where roots begin
greener than what they bring

the old people speak of death
frequently now
my grandmother speaks of those now
gone to spirit
now less than bone

# LEGON, GHANA, AFTER DARK

soft voices invisible serenade
from roadways, courtyards,
laughing trees & serene ponds palming
flat wide green leaves
holding incredibly loud bullfrogs
croaking over motion
of silent goldfish

Ga language sings over
darkening shadows mixing Akan where
English is pushed back into corners
of the language gumbo style

crickets orchestrate
their deafening oracular melodies,
blend high-life rhythms & C.K. Mann
with afro-sound of Fela Ransome Kuti
rumbling ground & a lonely
car horn

music, life's music,
punctuates the sweetness
of this beautiful modal cadence,
lifts the spirit into rare ecstasy

now listening to sculptors
of ancestral root music arranging
& rearranging their perfect chords
& octaves of discord & accord, dissonant
counterpoint eye begin to fall into the black
inkwell that leads to the egg-yoke
on the blue plate of God's table

fall into deep & untroubled sleep
at Akuafo Hall, at the University of Ghana
under rare dark incense showers under
rare dark incense showers

# GHANAIAN SONG—IMAGE

after rain
dark trees &
ghost shadows
sit upon
shoulders of
cotton mist

IGBOBI NIGHT;
*for Ron & Ellen Pulleyblank & Seyi Bajilayia*

dark fall
african masks
martell bottle
shadows
the wall    spider
in the corner
of the cognac
bottle a lone candle
burns on the table
invisible sounds
hum from imagbon
street climbs through
the open window
& love in
the heart will last
beyond distance
& time beyond
separation
of the grave

MEMORY

a lone candle
burning penetrating
the dark deepening
memory—pain
only a finger-
thought away


OUT HERE WHERE

out here where
the sky grows wings
the land is broad
& everywhere eye go
space holds me
within

## IT IS NOT

it is not who or what
you see
but how you see
it. the night.

the woman. the rhythm
of night lights going on.
off. in her face.
the smile of neon.
jewels on fingers.

the sound of ash
colliding with cotton.
the sound tears make falling
through blues. the voices.
guitar strings strummed
by silence. echoes.

echoes. gold-capped
dues of a mississippi black
man's grin. is. not who or what.
you see. but how.
you see it. thin.
or otherwise. deep.

this life is.
what you make of it. not
what you hope it to be. but
what it is. right or wrong.
what it is what you make it
to be it is right
or wrong. thin.
or otherwise. deep.
a blues. or its absence.
it is. a lyrical

rhythm. dissonant.
painting the night. the sound
of ashes. colliding with cotton.
is. how you hear it. feel it.
is. not what or who.
you either hear. or. you do
not hear. but how you hear
is the question here.

this poem. that gold-
capped blues. of that. black
man's grin. mississippi. is.
the sound tears make falling
through guitar strings.
colliding with cotton.

echoing bones
that lay screaming under-
water. under earth. is
the feeling you hear. chains.
is not what you see
but how you see it. death.
this life. is how you
make it. see it.

feeling. see it. hear
this life wedded to death.
see it. feeling. see it.

feeling. see it.
see. it.
hear. it.

## IN A SILENCE OF BELLS

in a silence of bells
& cardboard mackmen
round midnight
a screaming riot of trumpets
fork the suffocating hour

bones stretch
& are hands of time-clocks
beating hearts with no bodies
surrounding them stall in
an absence of rhythms

but eye come in on time
with no help from metronomes
picking bass strings of the night
but have forgotten
my subway token

so have to walk
the music all
the way home

# IN MEMORY OF BUNCHY CARTER

in this quick breath
of water spray airy
eye see your face
of light so darkly lit
through knifing
rain long gone friend
shadow of your tracking
tongue still moving
this pain of lost friend-
ship to call out your name
so distant now
so night grown green
under avalanches
of sunlight
& flowers

# THE OTHER NIGHT

the other brandy
sweetened night we was
kissin so hard & good
you sucked my tongue
right on out
my tremblin mouth
& eye had to
sew it back in
in order to tell
you about it

# FLYING KITES

*for Nathan Dixon, Friend & Poet*

1.

we used to fly kites
across skull-caps of hours
holes on blue wings
canvas of sinking suns eclipsed
winged eyes locked to wind
we'd cut the kite string away
the run them down blue tapestry
up the sky down again the sin-
king sun over
again the sinking sun

2.

now we fly words as kites
on winds through skies
as poems;
holy bloody sounds
ringing like eclipse
the sun's tongues

## TRANSFORMATION

catch the blues song
of wind in your bleeding
black hand, (w)rap it around
your strong bony fingers
then turn it into a soft-nosed pen
& sit down & write the love
poem of your life

## FIREFLIES

fireflies on night canvas
cat eyes glowing like moonbeams
climbing now towards hidden places
they speak to the language
of darkness & of their lives torn
from roots in flux & of their sub-
stance forming the core
substantially transparent they
swim through ethereal darkness
where silence can be wisdom
searching for open doors

# THE DAY DUKE RAISED:
## MAY 24TH, 1984

*for Duke Ellington*

1.

that day began with a shower
of darkness calling lightning rains
home to stone language
of thunderclaps shattering the high
blue elegance of space & time
a broken-down riderless horse
with frayed wings
rode a sheer bone sunbeam
road down into the clouds


2.

spoke wheels of lightning
spun around the hours high up
above those clouds duke wheeled
his chariot of piano keys
his spirit now levitated from flesh
& hovering over the music of most high
spoke to the silence
of a griot shaman/man
who knew the wisdom of God


3.

at high noon the sun cracked
through the darkness like a rifle shot
grew a beard of clouds on its livid bald
face hung down noon sky high
pivotal time of the flood-deep hours as duke
was pivotal being a five in the nine
numbers of numerology
as his music was the crossroads
the cosmic mirror of rhythmic gri-gri

4.

so get on up & fly away duke bebop
slant & fade on in strut dance swing riff
float & stroke those tickling gri-gri keys
those satin ladies taking the A train up
to harlem those gri-gri keys of birmingham
breakdown sophisticated
ladies mood indigo
so get on up & strut across gri-gri
raise on up your band's waiting


5.

thunderclapping music somersaulting
clouds racing across the blue deep wisdom
of God listen it is time for your intro
duke into that other place where the all-time
great band is waiting for your intro duke
it is time to make the music of God
duke we are listening for your intro
duke let the sacred music begin

# FOUR, AND MORE
*for Miles Davis*

I.

a carrier of incandescent dreams this
blade-thin shadowman stabbed by lightning
crystal silhouette
crawling over blues-stained pavements his life
lean he drapes himself his music across edges
his blood held tight within
staccato flights

clean as darkness & bright as lightning
reversed moments where the sound is two cat eyes
penetrating the midnight hours of moon pearls lacing
the broken mirrored waters
mississippi mean as a sun-drenched trumpet/man
holding dreams held high on any wind/light

voice walking on eggshells

2.

& time comes as the wrinkles
of your mother's skin shrinking inward
fly towards that compelling voice
light calling since time began
on the flip-side of spirit
you shed placentas at each stage of your music
then go down river exploring new blues

the drum skin of young years wearing down

the enigmatic search of your music
now your autumn years of shadows creeping twilight
dancers wrapped tight in cobwebs hold on
to one another

beneath fractured lights cracking the floor
their lives now prismatic poems at the point where the sun
disappears with every turning of the clock hands
spinning towards the death of light
there in the diamond point
of the river beyond the edges

the light glows smaller
grows inward becomes a seed to grow
another light illuminating the shadows
crystalline as this trumpetman

voice walking on eggshells

phosphorous as truth or blue
as luminescent water beneath the sun's eye

3.
O Silent Keeper of Shadows
of these gutted roads filled with gloomy ticking
of time-clocks/razor-bladed turnings of hairpin corners
of these irreducible moments of love found
when love was sought
iridescent keeper of rainbow laughter
arching out of broken-off gold-capped teeth

blues man holding the sun between his teeth

soothsayer of chewed-up moments
shekereman at the crossroads of cardinal points
talisman hanging from dewdrops singing deep
sea diver of transparent rhythmic poems

trumpet voice walking on eggshells

your shadow is as the river snake-thin
man at flood time blood lengthening in the veins
coursing through the earth's flesh

shaman man gone beyond the skies limit

music sleeps there in the riverbed
mississippi where those calcified shining bones sleep
deep reminding us of the journey from then to now
& from now to wherever it is we have to go

so pack your bags boy
the future is right around the corner
only a stone's throw from yesterday's/light

as is this carrier of afternoon dream music
trumpet voice walking on eggshells

this eggshell-walking trumpetman
voice hauntingly beautiful lyrical music man
gold as two cat eyes penetrating the midnight hours
as blood blackening the pavement mean music man
shadowman holding the night in the bell
of his trumpet singing

mississippi river pouring from roots of his eyes

4.
shadowman holding the night in his music
shekereman at the crossroads of cardinal points
elliptical talisman hanging from dewdrops singing
deep sea diver of haunting magical tones

trumpetman walking on eggshells

your shadow as the river at flood-time
snake-thin shaman man blade-sharp gone beyond
the sky's limit music sleeps there in your coursing
river veins curl around the bones
clear as diamond points on waters of sunsets

there where light grows inward
your genius moving out from that source
trumpetman walking on eggshells

afternoon dreamcarrier of blues in flight
steep night climber of haunting magical poems

juju hoodooman conjuring illuminating darkness

## SNAKE-BLACK SOLO

*for Louis Armstrong, Steve Cannon, Miles Davis, & Eugene Redmond*


with the music up high
boogalooin bass down way way low
up & under eye come slidin on in mojoin
on in spacin on in on a riff
full of rain
riffin on in full of rain & pain
spacin on in on a sound like coltrane

my metaphor is a blues
hot pain dealin blues is a blues axin
guitar voices whiskey broken niggah deep
in the heart is a blues in a glass filled with rain
is a blues in the dark
slurred voices of straight bourbon
is a blues dagger stuck off in the heart
of night moanin like bessie smith
is a blues filling up the wings
of darkness is a blues

& looking through the heart
a dream can become a raindrop window to see through
can become a window to see through this moment
to see yourself hanging around the dark
to see through
can become a river catching rain
feeding time can become a window
to see through

while outside windows flames trigger
the deep explosion
time steals rivers that go on & stay where they are
inside yourself moving soon there will be daylight
breaking the darkness

to show the way soon there will be voices breaking music
to come on home by down & up river breaking darkness
swimming up river the sound of louie armstrong
carrying riverboats upstream on vibratos
climbing the rain filling the rain
swimming up river
up the river of rain satchmo breaking the darkness
his trumpet & grin polished overpain speaking
to the light flaming off the river's back
at sunset snake river's back
river mississippi big muddy up from new
orleans to alton & east st. louis illinois
cross the river fron st. louis to come on home by
up river the music swims breaking silence of miles
flesh leaping off itself into space
creating music creating poems

now inside myself eye solo of rivers
catching rains & dreams & sunsets solo
of trane tracks screaming through night stark
a dagger in the heart solo
of the bird spreading wings for the wind
solo of miles pied piper prince of darkness
river rain voice now eye solo
at the root of the flower solo leaning voices
against promises of shadows soloing of bones
beneath the river's snake-back solo
of trees cut down by double-bladed axes
river rain voice now eye solo of the human condition
as blues solo of the matrix mojoin new blues solo
river rain voice now eye solo   solo

& looking through the heart a dream
can become a raindrop window to see through
can become this moment this frame to see through
to see yourself hanging
around the dark to see through this pain

can become even more painful as the meaning of bones
crawling mississippi river bottoms snakepits beneath
the snake-back solo catching rain catching time
& dreams washed clean by ajax

but looking through the dream can be
like looking through a clean window crystal
prism the night where eye solo now to be-
come the wings of night
to see through this darkness
eye solo now to become wings & colors
to become a simple skybreak shattering darkness
to become lightning's jagged sword-like thunder
eye solo to become to become
eye solo now to become to become

with the music up high
up way way high boogalooin bass down
way way low
up & under eye come slidin on in mojoin on in
spacin on in on a riff full of rain
river riff full of rain & trains & dreams
come slidin on in another riff
full of flames
leanin & glidin eye solo   solo
loopin & slidin eye solo now   solo

## POEM FOR
## SKUNDER BOGHASSIAN, PAINTER

music drumming skies
of your paintings of poetry
miles cookin there
with long gone trane leapin
canopies of distance

& space can be canvas
or bark negotiated by brushstrokes of silence

ghost evoking illusions of myth
wind-voice gongs
shaping shadows from mist

signatures that echo

# COLLAGE

wings of snow sweep
disintegrate
slow fall chimney ashes
belch through gray night
silently screaming

voices thick as molasses

blanket fluttering pavements
slide into one another
below moments
faces

ringing like bells

## MY POEMS HAVE HOLES SEWN
## INTO THEM

my poems have holes sewn into them
& they run searching for light
at the end of tunnels they become trains
or at the bottom of pits they become blackness
or in the broad winging daylight
they are the words that fly

& the holes are these words
letters or syllables with feathered wings
that leave their marks on white pages
then fly off like footprints tracked in snow
& only God knows where they go

this poem has holes stitched into it
as our speech which created poetry in the first place
lacerated wounded words that strike out original
meaning bleeding into language
hemorrhaging out of thick or thin mouths
has empty spaces & silences sewn into it

so my poems have holes sewn into them
& their voices are like different keyholes
through which dumb men search for speech blind
men search for sight
words like drills penetrating sleep
keys turning in the keyholes of language
like knives of sunrays stabbing blind eyes

my poems have holes sewn into them
& they are the spaces between words
are the words themselves
falling off into one another/colliding
like people gone mad they space out

fall into bottomless pits
which are the words

like silent space between chords of a piano
or black eyes of a figure in any painting
they fall back into themselves
into time/sleep
bottom out on the far side of consciousness
where words of all the world's poets go
& whisper in absolute silence

this poem has deep holes stitched into it
& their meanings have the deadly suck of quicksand
the irreversible pull of earth to any skydiver
the tortured pus-holes in arms of junkies

my poems have holes sewn into them
& they run searching for light at the end
of tunnels or at the bottom of yawning pits
or in the broad daylight where
the words flapping like wings of birds
fly whispering in absolute silence

# 4

---

FROM SKULLS ALONG THE RIVER, 1984

## SKULLS ALONG THE RIVER

*for my mother, Dorothy Marshall, and my father, Quincy Trouppe, Sr.*

1.

up from new orleans, on riverboats
from the gulf of mexico, memory carries
sweet legacy of niggerland speech, brown tongue bluesing
muddy water
underbottomed spirits crawling, nightmares
of shipwrecked bones, bones gone home to stone, to stone
bones gone home to stone, to stone
riverbottomed, underbellied spirits

bones gone home to stone, eye say
bones gone home to stone, eye say

skulls along the river

2.

& the faces of these faceless bones unknown
screaming arpeggios of stitched memory in cold light
cadences of blues
shrinking sun sprays shrieking with every turning
of black bone armed clocks

& it is the collected face of collected memory that wears
the metaphor of collected dust
the collected mathematics of lamenting calibrations
hieroglyphics
crackling & peeling & curling in stone, dust storms swirling
around edges
bones white as chiclet teeth in memory cloning
the images come locked in whatever
death there forever, forever locked in time
death there forever & forever locked
in time, in time

we suffer because we must
there is no other way to find beauty
there is no other way to find love
we suffer because we must
there is no other way home
to find the memory

& O the skeletons that have passed
my cracking eyeballs seeking true cadence
within the lamenting calibrations of music
history rattling dice bones
on their worn out knees
the already dead scraping earth, breath
for an even deeper death

the ultimate transmissioning migration

& O you midnight men of peppermint moons
rooster claw soliloquies raking at vision's corner
heroes emerging from sandblasted history books
grant me leather flesh of your weather worn wisdom
O blood-drenched gravediggers
anthractic soothsayers
O mellow prophets of crushed grapes & stomped berries
O grant me holy syllables of your blues laced tongues
perfect eardrums
O grant me sacred light of your blues
grant me sacred light of your blues
doowopping mackmen
grant me holy flight of your eagle—
winged life, O grant me the tongue of your blues
perfect eardrums, grant me holy flight
of your eagle-winged life
O grant me the tongue
of your blues perfect eardrums

3.

beginning now with the formless mystery of love
informing it all, cadences, its ritualized celebration
of birth as death as drama
its copacetic language of blues
inside the journey back under buzzard wings of parody
textures realized & lost & found & lost once again
the slitting, definitive answer
of a pearl handled razor hissing through
the dark's wailing wall mystery, of flesh
wallowing in its own gluttony
inside the breath of death?

now hear the hieroglyphics of space & time forming
sculpting in winds from great distances, voices
shapes down way way low, voices
taking on colors, turning around & taking on shape
voices spinning into blurring faces swimming
trying to breach this calligraphy
of space & time & distance

voices, down way way low, spinning themselves
into memory phono-discs, voices as faces
down way way low, way way low
voices spinning & turning into faces in memory
phono-discs, down way way low, down
way, way low

send back now the memory further back than bone
see there, now, the polished stones lifted
& singing, singing

becoming birds that are words
their wings being the holy myths that fill up our lives
with movement, movement
now, listen to the blood burning songs breaking
through & into our rivervoiced veins

climbing toward the plateau
of the heart

listen to the rains
beating against the underbelly of those stones
marking worm deep earth bottoms where
the narcissus of flesh

rests

listen to windtongues
drums now breaking into flames & wind trumpet songs
opening up doorways to rivers, listen now
to hearts, listen
to rhythms of stones, beating hearts climbing
towards the dark, listen to rhythms
your soon to be calcified
worm eaten heart
listen now

listen now, to the dark

    4.
we are the dark
are dark stitched voices climbing
memories from the heart, are secret
arpeggios of spirit
scaling towards the light
voices of weeping rains, teardrops
hanging from history, eyelids
of that toad squatting city
by the mississippi river

wide spread arms of slippery catfish
deep inside skulls of mississippi
river nights born of savage flights
are dark, hip voices, stitched

into fabric of those razor
bladed nights
blues kneeling down
eye say blues kneeling down
before that packing house city
wide spread arms slippery as cat
fish, spirits climbing towards
the cracks of moonbeams
slashed light, blues
kneeling down, moonbeams
climbing towards cracks
slashed light


   5.

O sweet lovers of no faces

of all races with desert bone dry eyes
of no reception
                    pain knee deep in quicksand
who give sandpaper tongues of no sweetness
kisses cold as piranha teeth
eyes digging scaly reflections in dirty mirrors
cracked & fading
become now a confluence of rivers, blood
a confluence of musical faces, blood swimming through
sundown, dusk, blood, the sonorous magic of elliptical
calibrations spinning inside
memory discs, blood
stitched into music

sing now, of windprints, birds
climbing cadences, stitched memory
sing now of rapture swimming through river-veins
spirit of bones bright as lightning in blood
deep mud beds of mississippi river bottoms
where the ancestors sing now in sleep
sing now a bone deep rhapsody

a memory of skulls
blues steeped

sing now stone-sculptured
legacy, of blues chiseled mornings
sing now, sing now

sing a blues

6.

but this road back long gone again long
gone, back again blues
long gone eye come back forward again, to this
river mississippi, to this toad squatting city
catfish arms widespread in slippery welcome
come back home again

                          to these dry-bone kisses
formaldehyde memories, eyes death ridden
as forty-five bullets

come back home again carrying my age strapped
on my side like a revolver
all my young quicksilver years running into this river
mississippi river, snake-back carrier of dreams
& home is wherever ancestor bones are
buried kneedeep memories live as dreams
become ribcages of miracles
built from death
as a man holding the sun between his teeth

his smile a dazzling daybreak, a blue-black blues man
sun man caught the sun between his gapped teeth
sprouted wings & flew away into the music
now his spirit holds up the sky
his smile the golden eye
torching high, morning skies

snake-back carrier of dreams, mississippi
seven throw eleven to win at the game of dice
eye carry snake-back river of dreams on my back
river mississippi, where the spirits climb out
of now, move beneath the arch's
parabolic flight
upside down question mark
razor's edge of a stationary pendulum slashing
the blue throat of sky turning now
a skillet fried yellow now

snake-back carrier of dreams the song climbs
out of itself now, shaking riverweeds that turn
into faces familiar on memory discs, spinning
faces familiar as crushed coal
dust, greets me here
with outspread arms filigreeing cobwebbed drapes
old streets where familiar buildings have been
removed, like abscessed teeth from the mouth
of old fisherman ghoul
who used to tell me all those great stories
of the heydays of st. louis, before the scars came
before the mumbles came & he lost his peg-leg teeth
like those abscessed buildings
before he fell into senility & was pulverized
by the pendulum wrecking ball of progress
that is time, which is history's
consuming fire, which is death
& life at the same time

7.

but this road that has been so long gone now
is here again, back again blues
long gone eye have come back to this muddy river
again, to this toad squatting city of catfish arms
widespread in slippery welcome
come back home again

to all my quicksilver memories running
into this river, mississippi river
snake-back carrier of dreams

river mississippi

snake-back carrier of dreams
seven throw eleven eye win
at the game of dice
seven throw eleven eye win whatever
the game holds for me now
whatever this catfish armed city
holds for me now, eye win if only
eye can come back & go forward again
at the same time, seven throw eleven
eye win at the game
of dice & the blues

snake-back carrier of dreams

seven throw eleven eye win
the blues, seven throw eleven

eye win the blues

## SOUTH CENTRAL
## VANDENTER STREET RUNDOWN

To leave any house
was to smell the scent,
burnt flesh scent hanging
noxious in the air,
& to leave any house
was to know the odor,
burnt flesh hanging
like death in the air,
burnt flesh hanging
like death in the air

& to know the odor
was to know
where death came from,
packin house slaughter house
burnin flesh blues,
spreadin the news 'bout death,
burnin flesh,
spreadin the news 'bout death

& can smell it in springtime,
can smell it in summertime,
can smell it
seven days a week singeing air,
in autumntime, in wintertime,
all the time anytime,

burnt flesh hanging
a death in the air,
burnt flesh hanging
as death in the air

RIVER TOWN PACKIN HOUSE BLUES
*for Sterling Brown*


Big Tom was a black nigguh man,
cold & black,
eye say Big Tom was a black nigguh man,
black steel flesh,
standin like a gladiator, soaked in
animal blood, bits of flesh,
wringin wet,
standin at the center of death,
buzzards hoverin, swingin his hammer called death,
260 workdays,
swingin his hammer named death

Big Tom was a black packin houseman,
thirty years,
eye say Big Tom was a black packin houseman,
loved them years,
& swang his hammer like ol John Henry
poundin nails,
swang that hammer twenty years
crushin skulls
of cows & pigs screamin fear,
the man underneath slit their throats,
twenty years,
the man underneath slit their throats

Big Tom was a 'prentice for ten long years,
watchin death,
eye say Big Tom was 'prentice for ten long years,
smellin death,
was helper to a fat white man,
who got slow,
was helper to a fat white man,
who swang a hammer

till he couldnt do it no mo,
so he taught Big Tom how to kill
with a hammer,
he taught Big Tom how to kill

& twenty years of killin
is a lot to bring home,
eye say twenty years of killin
is a lot to bring home,
& drinkin too much gin & whiskey
can make a gentle/man blow
dont chu know
eye say drinkin too much
gin & whiskey
can make a good man
sho nuff blow,
dont chu know

Big Tom beat his wife after killin all day,
his six chillun too,
eye say Tom beat his wife after killin all day,
his young chillun too,
beat em so awful bad, he beat em right out dey shoes,
screamin blues,
eye say he beat em so awful bad
he made a redeyed hungry alley rat spread the news
'bout dues
these black/blues people was payin, couldnt even bite em,
cause of the dues
these black/blues people was payin

But Tom killed six men, maimed a couple a hundred,
& never served a day,
eye say Big Tom killed six men, maimed a couple a
hundred,
never in jail one day,
the figures coulda been higher, but the smart ones,

they ran away,
eye say the number that was maimed, or dead, coulda
been higher,
but the smart ones,
they ran away, swallowin pride, saved from the graveyard,
another day,
the smart ones,
they ran away

Big Tom, workin all day, thirty years,
uh huh, sweatin heavy
Big Tom swingin his hamma, all right, twenty summers
outta love
Big Tom killin for pay,
Uh huh, twenty autumns, outta need,
Big Tom dealin out murders, like a houseman, all night,
in the painyards, outta false pride,
Big Tom drinkin heavy, uh huh,
laughing loose in taverns,
Big Tom loose
In Black communities, death fights cancels light,
& Big Tom keeps on, stumbling

& twenty years of killin
is too much to bring home to love,
eye say twenty years of killin
is too much to bring home to love,
& drinkin heavy gin & whiskey
can make a strong man fall in mud,
eye say drinkin too much/ gin & whiskey
can make a good man have bad blood
dont chu know
can make a strong
man have
bad blood

Big Black Tom was a cold nigguh man,
strong & black,
eye say Big Black Tom was a cold nigguh man,
hard steel flesh,
& stood like a gladiator, soaked in blood,
bits of flesh,
soakin wet,
stood at the center, in the middle of death,
sweatin vultures,
swingin his hamma called death, 260 workdays,
twenty years,
like ol John Henry,
eye say swingin his hammer named death

# POEM FOR MY BROTHER TIMMY

We walked streets
of river-rhythm town counting
cars that passed
for nothing else better to do
warm cold days now packed
away in straw

& when at home on Delmar
& Leonard streets, living over Joe's
Super Market, on weekends
would repeat from our window
the same ritual
all over again

this counting of passing cars
(you took the Fords
eye took the Chevrolets
but the Cadillacs would win.)

& from our window on saturday nights
we would watch the drunken fights
across the street
at Meyer's tavern
where people died with
ridiculous ease from street surgeons' knives

Summers brought picnics &  barbecues
baseball games & hot funky parties
where we styled hard laid off
in bad summer rags

& on warm idle days
on concrete playground courts
eye would beat the hell out of you
playing basketball until it got dark

In winter, we would bundle up tight
in fast shrinking clothes
bought three years before
when daddy was making money playing baseball
in Batista's Cuba, or bought when
mother was working downtown being
a deskclerk at Sonnenfeld's

& on frozen winter nights
we would fight like two vicious alley cats
over who pulled the cover off of who
afterwards, we would sleep side by side
in the dark in our own spilt blood

& if someone was ever foolish enough
to mess with either one of us
they had to contend with the both
of us sho-nuff righteously stompin
eleven-thousand corns on their
                              sorry asses

But time has worn away those days
as water rubs smooth in time
                    a rough & jagged stone

You took the blues of those days
filled with sun dues & blood & turned them
into rhythms you played
superbly on your talking drums
before you heard the calling of your Lord sanctified

Eye took that beautiful song
you gave to me & turned into poetry
this poem eye give to you now

with a brother's deep love

# OLD BLACK LADIES ON BUS STOP CORNERS

*for my grandmother, Leona Smith*


*Blue black and bow bent under beautiful*
*Blue black and bow bent under beautiful*
*Blue black and bow bent under beautiful*

& it never did matter
whether the weather
was flame tongue licked
or as cold as a well digger's asshole
in late December when santa claus
was working his cold money bullshit
that made financiers grin
all the way to secret bank vaults
overflowing with marble eyes
of third world children

*Blue black and bow bent under beautiful*
*Blue black and bow bent under beautiful*
*Blue black and bow bent under beautiful*

never did matter
whether the days were storm raked
with lightning steaked clouds
tornados skipping crazy
to their own savage beat
shooting hailstone death
at the skulled sunken eyes
of tired old ladies
tired old black ladies
standing on bus stop corners
pain wrapped as shawls around their necks

*Blue black and bow bent under beautiful*
*Blue black and bow bent under beautiful*
*Blue black and bow bent under beautiful*

& "Mama" it didn't matter
that pain scarred feet overworked
numb legs bow bent under beautiful
grew down out of old worn dresses
seemingly fragile    gauntly skeletal frail
as two old mop sticks    scarecrow legs
didn't matter cause you stood there anyway
defying nature's chameleon weather—
defying all reason
stood there testifying over 400 years
of madness & treason

*Blue black and bow bent under beautiful*

No, it didn't matter
cause the beauty of your heroic dimensions
grown lovely in twisted swamps
grown lovely from desolate land
grown pure & full from wombs
of concrete blood & bones
of concrete blood & bones & death
of death & sweat chained to breath
didn't matter dark proud flower
scrubbed by age & cold & rain
the foreign name given your father
swaying body high up there in the burning breeze

*Blue back and bow went under beautiful*

cause you stood there anyway
unforgettably beautiful in your standing
work scarred black lady
numb legs & bow bent under beautiful
stood there on pain scarred feet overworked
numb legs and bow bent under beautiful
under the image of your father
swaying high up there in the burning breeze

{ *119* }

now sweet music     love sings soft calm
soft beauty from your washed aging windows—
giving us strength
                        during these mad, bizarre days

No, it didn't matter
Whether the weather was flame tongue
licked or as cold as a well digger's asshole
in late December
Cause you stood there anyway
in full bloom
of your strength and rare beauty
& we have learned to love your life
& will vindicate the pain of your life
the memory of your father
who is also our great grandfather
with the foreign name & who sways high up there over your legs
blue black & bow bent under beautiful
the weight of 400 years carried
of blood and bones and death in mud
of breath & sweat chained to death
                                        numb legs & bow bent under beautiful
the image of your father swaying high
up there in the burning breeze

              didn't matter whether the weather was flame-tongue-licked
or as cold as a well digger's asshole in late december
cause you stood there anyway
flowering in full beauty
& made us strong

*Blue black and bow bent under beautiful*
*Blue black and bow bent under beautiful*
*Blue black and bow bent under beautiful*

## RIVER RHYTHM TOWN

River rhythm town
under sun / moon laughter.
river blues town filled
with blues people
doin' blues dues thangs

cycles of shinin laughter

listenin to dues sounds everyday
of Chuck Berry      Miles Davis
Little Richard      The Dells
Thelonious Monk
& John Coltrane

Walkin the hip walk,
wearin the hip new thangs,
laid off clean as a broke dick dog
in the cut,
chasin hot black girls down
rhythm & blues,
doin the belly grind in corners
of smoke filled red lighted
funky parties

music risin hot
between cold funk
of wall to wall
partyin black shadows

weavin spinnin dancin
drinkin in the beauty of sensuous
black foxy ladies
yea!
rubbin thrills against pain

of imprisoned skin screamin for release
from overworn tight-fittin fabrics
& eye remember smiles
dazzling as daybreak,
& soft as mother's
warm embracing eyes

eye remember love
in the grass sweating as rivers
from our fused flesh

eye remember thrills
eye remember smiles
eye remember love
in the grass sweating as rivers

from our fused flesh

eye remember sadness

eye remember St. Louis,
river rhythm town under
sun/moon laughter,
river blues town filled
with blues people
doin blues dues thangs

& eye remember death
shattering as daybreak

## ST. LOUIS NEIGHBORHOOD;

*for Lester Bowie, trumpet player & john hicks, piano player*

1.

night swept down here sometimes with a cape of screams
& eye remember my mother's voice insistent with instructions
above the bedlam, instructive with the memory of ironing cords
punctuating their hissing electrical language
cutting through tense space to (w)rite signatures
cross my back deadly as razors slitting
in the name of love, in the name of love

2.

slicing imagination quicks clean through to bone
swift as solo hits of a silent sadist/rapist
alone inside shadowed wings of darkness
destruction loose & remembered
as a rabid dog's foam drips singular

drop by drop, echoing replicas replicate
& who prowl dracula fantasies & werewolf delusions
frankenstein tanna leaves, mummified traumas
bullet death blown clean through dreams
the brain reamed & picked

now it is a seam of darkness

3.

but there are collard green memories of sundays here too
bright warm weekdays where we sashayed lace through with rituals
passive sometimes feelings splashed with colors, laidback hesitation
& sometimes there were those who came close to the meaning
of yardbird parker, miles davis & bud powell
like you, lester bowie & john hicks
moved past what was told you you must become
became cock of the walks, bright stride of trumpet

genius & piano keys gliding wherever fingers told them to
conversations stitched into laughter cascading sounds
& rhythms kissing profound as hardons
mysterious as birth & great brass breath
breathed over black & white ivory keys

closing up the distance after miles & bud

# WHOSE DEATH IS THIS WALKING

whose death is this walking towards me now
eye know it's not mine, eye left mine
behind, back at the undertaker's

so who belongs to this corpse that just passed
me now, wagging a st. james version of the bible
or was it a readers digest version

look, his eyes are black & flat as crushed
shadows, deep as hot tar pits
whose corpse is this walking towards me

now, eye know it's not mine—
eye left mine behind
back at the cemetery

## THE SKY EMPTIES DOWN ICE

the sky empties down ice
winter grows quickly in your face
of crowded ashtrays

you say
you have come this far for cigarettes
fun & a warm adventure
in bed
but your razor nails
clawing my back
tell me

another story

meanwhile    the sea whispers
rapture on the other side of time
pigeons drop slimy
shit into
your vanilla ice cream cone

but don't get angry
just yet

just because this moment defies
gravity    takes off & lands
just there
where a fart just left

all eye know is this

the sky is emptying down ice
& winter is growing quickly in your face
of crowded ashtrays

in your butt-end face

of crowded ashtrays

# HALLOWEEN PARADE IN GREENWICH VILLAGE, 1978

it was the night of your funeral     mama
the ritualized mourning night of your death
& at the head of the affair
a black man selling luminous green bracelets of light
then a space man     plastic arrows flashing on & off
a richard nixon double stalks in clown costume
rubber face     long curled-up harlequin
shoes     juggles silver balls
as dracula bites at a young girl's neck
on bleecker street     eggheads bobbing up & down
skeletons grinning gyrating bones     saxophones
wailing deep in the unreal noise
conga drums underneath the muffled night
pulsating tight runs as tambourines
rattle the drunk & staggering night

now fabulous masks pop out of the crowd
like champagne powered corks     cold-cock eyeballs
of people     sequins waving cat-tails     funny witches
rake long silver fingernails     transmit light
dance up & down fire
escapes up side walls of buildings drowning
& saturated in rainbowed flights of color
sight octopus like twenty-foot gondolas
of silk jitterbugging the night
as a pig in a red satin dress switches
her oversized rubber-packed poontang quivers
a trembling tall wolfman on stilts shivers
two styrofoam black gloves
hold moon faces of two uptight men-girls
framed like twin sunflowers in their plucking fingers
a flute choir floats rhythms over space & sights
two screaming homos swapping spit
crossing seventh avenue south the parade claws

traffic packed ten blocks back in the night
honking its whining anger

slide now down greenwich street
hook a left on west tenth    pass patchin place
(time keeping the heart of the energy) moving
past jefferson market library
which used to be a church & before that on the other
side of time    the old women's clocked high tower
of detention    where angela davis once looked out
& down from on molasses cheering crowds—
old-time ritualized masturbations—
but where now    mama
& on the night of your funeral    mama
the ritualized hour of your death
a gigantic spider waves its eight legs
then folds them back over its abdomen    mama
beneath the cheese-faced dial of the high
tower clock    mama    where black hands still turn
around time but where now this gigantic gyrating spider
mama is gripping its eight legs around the church spire
mama    appears to make love    shivers in climax
mama    turns voices into agitated flights

now the drums move away carrying the spirit
hubbub of the thing unrecognized that holds us here
past peter's backyard charcoal room
in front of which
a two-headed pig holds titties of a possessed dracula girl—
cackling like that clawing hissing girl thing in *The Exorcist*—
while the two-headed pig thing mounts & begins humping her
with a four foot rubber penis
a sing-song man with a t.v. for a head screams;
*give me your money*
*give me all your dreams & money*
*eye sell sleek cars guaranteed to fall apart in three years*
*sell sewing machines    poison eye stitch into your ears*

*& eyes    sell bona-fide illusions    packaged mannerisms*
*just for your use    give me money*
*give me all of your dreams & money*
*1984 has arrived*


now the drums up ahead call us to turn    mama
at fifth avenue    rip van winkle on roller skates
& dressed in orange black & purple cruises by
sashaying    the parade laid dead now in the cut of its own rhythm
moves past feathers now
(above which the fine lady from mississippi lived over once
before she moved in with yours truly & blew her final chance of staying
a swinging young bachelorette)
comes to washington square park    on top of whose  spotlighted    lookalike
champs-elysee gateway    perches a red-suited devil waving blessings
like the pope welcoming everybody to the final destruction
of this american bacchanalia


now television cameras roll their shadow-catching eyes
prop lights splash darkness to the bone with light


a beggar drags by pre-arranged rags
two more fags in rock drag fall out with one another
scream at each other over whose tongue tastes the sweetest
while a latin band warms up the square with salsa
languaging the park
spirit runners slip in & out of the dark
mounting rhythms lovers lock themselves to flesh
richard nixon's double-take juggles silver balls
bad as rubber checks
the band leaps into burning salsa
sways the people    cooks & turns passion
into joy on the very edge of frenzy
rockets go off in the sky of margaret's eyes
whose smile is a kiss
as a ten-foot-high silk dragon with people for legs
rides by stunning night air above rhythms the crowd is dancing

holy inside salsa spirits moving away inside themselves
while outside the park a pale man in white lace
directs traffic with a jeweled conductor's baton
rollers under his hairnet yawn open
their gulping mouths looping
bleached blond arrogance

now at the end of the strange affair     mama
the black man still jaw-jacking selling green bracelets
of light     ringing corded necks     as the weird man
with the t.v. for a head is still screaming
we fall out of the dying confusion into the restaurant
*volare* which means in italian *to fly*
eye ease on up next to margaret
climb through the love she carries in her eyes
leave the strange evening behind
enter *volare*'s soft candlelit rhythms
simmer the magic down mama with a kiss
on the night of your funeral     mama
on this halloween night you were laid to rest

# EIGHTH AVENUE POEM

on eighth avenue
between 116th and
121st streets
some of the junkies
have feet so bad
they could step
on a dime
and tell you
whether it's
heads or tails

# POEM FOR LADY DAY & DINAH WASHINGTON

there is nothing but yawning space between
us now, lady day, dinah washington
queens of the blues, your memories breaking stillness
the octaves of your genius voices razing where
silence reconstructs itself
is pregnant punctuation of absence between chords
a hesitation of sound, arrested like speech
of a revolutionary nailed to a star
your memories of eyes & slurs
bending around your sicknesses fill us with omens
we know is nothing but indigo-blues stabbed
with light deepening between us now
like sorrow, your voices of broken necks twisting
black men lynched, slurs through your muddy syllables
flowing like the mississippi river over bright
bones black flesh used to wrap itself around once
your voices of highways & night trains
blues with dead men & heroin
secret as the voice in the moon of gin bottles
filling this awesome stillness of empty rooms
the octaves of your memories scaling—
silence reconstructing itself, stillborn—
in this indigo new absence, your voices
punctuating between chords, becoming syllables
the image of your voices in memory
full of omens, like your sad, beautiful
faces rooted in this american apocalypse of blues
rooted in this american apocalypse of blues

## IMAGE

within the murmuring of darkness
silence grows wings of shadows
locked between cued spaces of syllables
the moon contemplates its own distance
from itself, yawns from the breath
of God, nails itself
deep in black, shimmering velvet—
a rune-pearl replacing the sun
after trembling sundown runs
after trembling sundown runs

## RIFF

may days bring an explosion of music
bouncing off edges, walls, poly rhythms
nodding sad junkies seducing daddy death
swinging around corners, cool breezes
floating, touching everything
love left whispering now, new shadows
crisscrossing connections tucked away
in memory, winter yielding, spring
resurrects all things possible
& the sun laughing always on the run

## IMPRESSIONS 3

along shadow roads mojoin rhythms clear
toned bell tone karintha dusks bleed
carry along the guitar of memory

sea red moons in fingers of trees
owl hoot hootin blue-black train whistles hear
ghosts in the canebrake leaves
blinking eyes swimming
fireflies breathing fire rhythms, hear winds
carried along by drums

heart throbs of nights muffled bass language
runs through keys—holes—
carrying ancient blood over distances

opening up music, fusing new-old rhythms
gospel choirs jazzographying these leaves
mojoin drums hummin
carried along by karintha dusks/needs

mojoin drums hummin voodoo
carried along by blue keys runnin

# IMPRESSIONS 8

american lawrence welk
saturdays
            football games
hot dogs & falstaff beer
chased by fire
of bourbon

mcdonalds & a&p
sears bank of america
crackers
in chicken noodle soup
ivory snow liquid
miss america kentucky fried
palmolive dove
commercials

madison avenue
cowboys
            hillbilly black
militant japtalians
niggindians hungericans
mestizos mulattoes
quadroons

slick hip stylin spirits
of the greased way highsign
give high fives of speech
step the low road
strut bojangle
their words in motion
prancing say "gimme some skin
lay a fin on me" confront
soda crackers
in this gumbo soup

chaos of conflicting
dreams this
american gumbo
soup of chaos
& conflicting dreams

## IMPRESSIONS 12

buck dance antlers frozen
in the still air
like fingers gripping death
by the side of the crooked road
a young deer dropped down
in its tracks
assumes a praying position
a bullet hole in the middle
of its shocked
forehead

IMPRESSIONS 15


bright day in pennsylvania
steel blue
        the mountains clear
from here & out hear cold
the naked sky
soft at duskglow when the sun
sinks clear down

through winter trees bare
skin leaves shake down

        snow mounds cover
the ground & footprints
like inked words on white pages
print themselves
into snow

stretch themselves around
& into dark, awesome
silence, grows
into worlds

# JUST CRUISIN & WRITIN

Writin poems
while cruising
at seventy miles
per hour
on the pennsylvania
turnpike
can be spiritual
fun
if you don't
run into
anyone

## MEETING

again time shaped for eclipse
suddenly designed & shaped
into a moment

that we are drawn to each other
is beyond all question

so what it all boils down to
is can we mix ourselves
into this moment
of sweetness

luxuriating as love
lathering down as magic
tonguing seconds

sink purring
into time's sweat

# HARLEM LATE NIGHT LYRIC

trucks growl these iced empty streets
as do voices fleet silence punctuates in flight
stabbing screams of death
pharaoh blows through his saxophone light
some carry as lodes of memory the language of tradition replaced
by catastrophic absences
the awesome muted hush of talking drums

where then the machinery of benevolence predicted
where the infant rose of new breath opening as a fertile womb
was promised once somewhere back in all those doctored scriptures
a seeding sun disguised perhaps
is what was promised us in autumn

now winter reminds spring is just off-stage
recharging love perhaps then will arrive—enter rooms—
lovelier than the fragrance of fresh-cut roses
the swelling of sweet tongues lathered in saliva

the cooing of birds skying through eyes

# THE DAY STRIDES THERE ON THE WIND
*for Leo Maitland*

the day strides there on the wind
its wings are the people's thoughts
breath contains
& finally, it is the speech of God
that shapes everything

that brash shouting trumpet
leaping out of a window, somewhere
that lonely saxophone woman, walking
there, in your most erotic, imagination
the books opened & closed
that tell us nothing
but what they are

these smells from hidden kitchens
emerging from other smells
to surround our nostrils with incense
to show & tell everything that you are
is most things but standing up naked

& so we wrap ourselves up
in illusions, wear the mask that dunbar
spoke of, wrap our dreams up in dreams
of others, who never know what
to do with their own
& so we sit watching patches of light
falling through the hairdos of trees

still, the day strides there on the wind
& its wings are the people's thoughts
that it contains
& finally, it is the speech
of God that shapes everything

# MEMOS & BUTTONS

he couldn't even spell albuquerque
had tuna fish garlic breath
mixed in with cigarettes & a job way beyond
his capacity
he was a bona fide ten-martini man over lunch
same exact thing during rush hours
walking around
with a copper wire for a brain
someone was sending
morse code to

he was a modern man of technology
read the wall street journal & forbes
religiously every day
commuting on suburban trains with spittin'
images cloning himself, locked in
& giggling for xerox, texas instruments
ibm, hadn't read a deep book
in God knows when
computer printouts being his bible

found himself thinking one day
of murdering his invalid wife, widowed
mother & three teenaged children

he was a modern, western man of technology
carried his mind around locked up
in a leather brief case

liked to push memos & buttons

# POEM REACHING TOWARDS SOMETHING

we walk through a calligraphy of hats slicing off foreheads
ace-deuce cocked, they slant, razor sharp, clean
through imagination, our spirits knee-deep in what we have forgotten
entrancing our bodies now to dance, like enraptured water lilies—
my memory & me—the rhythm in liquid stride of a certain look—
rippling eyeballs through breezes—
riffling choirs of trees where a trillion slivers of sunlight prance
across filigreeing leaves, a zillion voices of bamboo reeds
green with summer's saxophone burst
wrap themselves, like transparent prisms of dew—
drops around images, laced with pearls & rhinestones
perhaps it is through this, or in the decoding of syllables
that we learn speech, that sonorous river of broken mirrors
carrying our dreams, assaulted by pellets of rain-
drops, the prisons of words entrapping us between parentheses—
two bat wings curving into cynical smiles

still, there is something here that needs explaining beyond
the hopelessness of miles, the light at the end of the midnight tunnel—
some say it is a train coming right at us—
where do the tumbling words spend themselves after they have spent
all meaning residing in the warehouse of language
after they have slipped like smoke
from our lips, where do the symbols they carry stop everything
put down roots, cleanse themselves of everything but clarity—
though here eye might be asking a little too much of any poet's head
full as it is with double-entendres

still, there are these hats slicing foreheads off in the middle
of crowds, the calligraphy of this penumbra slanting
ace-deuce cocked, carrying the perforated legacy of bebop, these bold
peccadillo, pirouetting pellagras, razor-sharp-clean, they cut
into our rip-tiding dreams carrying their whirlpooling imaginations

their rivers of schemes assaulted by pellets of rain-
drops, these broken mirrors reflecting sonorous
words entrapping us between parentheses—
two bat wings curved, imprisoning the world

## LAS CRUCES, NEW MEXICO;

*for Keith Wilson, Donna Epps Ramsey, Andrew Wall, Charles Thomas & Thomas Hocksema*


the high, great mesas, flat as vegas gambling tables
rock-hard, as red dust swirls into miniature tornados
dancing down roads red with silence, as these
faces of solitary indians, here where white men quick-tricked
their way to power with houdini bibles, hidden agendas
of bullets & schemes of false treaties

& black men alone here in this stark high place of mesquite
bushes, white sand mountains, colors snapped in incredible
beauty, eyes walking down vivid sunsets, livid purple scars slashing
volcanic rock, tomahawking language scalping this ruptured space
of forgotten teepees, so eye listen to a coyote wind
howling & yapping across the cactused, dry high vistas
kicking up skirts of red dirt at the rear end of quiet houses

squatting like dark frogs & crows, etched silhouettes high on live
wires popping speech, caw-cawing in the sand-blasted wind
stroked trees, caw-cawing all over the mesilla valley

& here along the rio grande river, dry, parched tongue bed, snaking
mud, cracked & dammed north in the throat of albuquerque
mescalara, zuni, apache & navaho live here,
scratch out their firewater
breath, peyote
secret eyes roaming up & down these gaming table mesas
their memory dragging chains through these red breathing streets
while geronimo's raging ghost haunts their lives with what they did
not do, stretching this death strewn history back to promises
& hope, a hole in the sky, a red omen moon
where death ran through
like water whirlpooling down a sink

& this shaman moon blown here a red target of light, at the end
of a tunnel of blackness, where a train speeds through now
towing breaknecking flights of light, where daybreak sits wrapped around
a quiet, ancient navaho, wrapped in cosmic, american colors, sits
meditating these scorched, white sands, flat
distant high mesas, shaped like royal, "Basotho Hats," chili peppers, churls
pecan groves, roadrunner, chaparral birds, salt cedars sprouting
parasitic along bone, white ditches, bordering
riverbeds thirsting for water
meditates these wide, flat, black lava-rocks
holding strange imprints of fossilized speech that died
before they knew what hit them, as did those silent
clay faced ancestors of this solitary navaho wrapped in breaking
colors, bursting sunlight, meditating the lay of this enchanting
blues land, changing its face every mile or so

& in their faces indians carry the sadness of ancestors
who wished they had listened to those long gone
flaming words—battlecries!—of geronimo, whose screaming ghost
prowls these bloody, muddy streets, baked dry now by the flaming eye
torching the sky, wished they had listened instead of chaining
his message in these coyote, howling winds
kicking up skirts of dirt
whose language yaps like toothless old men & women
at the rear-end of quiet houses, whose lights dance slack
at midnight, grow black & silent as death's worn-out breath
beneath these pipe-organ mountains, bishop's peaked
caps holding incredible silence, here
in the mesilla valley

where the rio grande river runs dry
its thirsty spirit dammed north in the throat of albuquerque
at the crossroads of fusion & silence, in the red gush swirls—
whispering litanies sawblading through ribcages, dust memory—
snaking winds over the mesilla valley brings
long-gone words of geronimo
haunting, las cruces, new mexico
long-gone wind, whispering, geronimo, geronimo

## IT ALL BOILS DOWN

it all boils down to a question of what
anything is being done for, in the first place
a reason, perhaps, stronger than the pull of any
magnet, perhaps, the first recognition
of clouds cruising through seas of blue
breath, shaped like battleships

on the other hand, it could be a fascination wearing
rings on sweating, claw-like fingers
something we have forgotten, knew nothing about ever
like the future of a question only time holds answers to
such as the exact moment death puts a lean on flesh, perhaps
& the thin suit vanity wears collapses
in on itself as the spirit takes leave of breath
& voices swell into a cacophonous blues, mother

somewhere in all of this there are connections fusing
something, perhaps, in the mellifluous
nodding of crazed junkies—that sad colony of leprous, popeye feet & hands—
is a dance, a catatonic premonition of unheeded weather reports
like knowing somewhere deep
eclipsed suns will perhaps experience joy
in the shaved light—

a shopping list of syllables is what poets carry
when confronting the winds of language
beyond that only the wind knows what it is doing—
like evil laughter gleaming machetes swing under streetlamps
slicing quick words that cut a man too short to shit sometimes, perhaps
a concertino stream of blue ragas when
breath flies suddenly back here, mysterious, as in those moon glinting
eyes fixed in silence, the dime-polished speech of felines
in a midnight moment of celebration

a bone dry squawking hawk talking away up there
suddenly, beyond dues, disappearing into blue quicksand
flapping wings of questions unanswered

down here, it all boils down to questions
ribcages pose & leave scattered under terrifying suns
on desert floors, the timeless, miraging sands holding
light, the steaming, seamless language
in flight & flowing into midnight

moons climbing between me & you

## 116TH STREET & PARK AVENUE

*for Victor Hernández Cruz & Pedro Pietri*


116th street fish smells, pinpoint la marqueta
up under the park avenue, filigreed viaduct
elevated tracks
where graffitied trains run over language
there is a pandemonium of gumbo colors stirring up
jumbalaya rhythms
spanish harlem, erupting
street vendors on timbale sidewalks
where the truth of things is what's happening now
que pasas on the move, andale
worlds removed from downtown, park avenue gentry, luxury coops
where latino doormen just arrived smile their *tip me good,*
*tip me good, tip me good* greetings
opening doors
carry their antediluvian rice & bean villages, old world
style, dripping from zapata moustaches
shaped perfect as boleros,
their memories singing images underneath shakespearean
cervantes balconies, new world don juans
smelling of cubano cigars, two broken tongues
lacing spanglish up into don q syllables, cuba libre
thick over sidewalks, voices
lifted & carried up into dance
up into mambo cha cha slick steps, these bodies
imagine themselves to be ballroom floors
rumbling car horns, palmieri fused
machito fired, pacheco tuned, barretto drums
bolero guitars wiring morse code puns, root
themselves back in villages
of don juan, romeo,
zapata, marti, in cuba writing poetic
briefs under cigar trees, the lingua-franca
of nicolas guillen, morejon, cruz & pietri

laying down expressions of what's happening now
& weaved through this pandemonium of gumbo
colors up under
the park avenue, filigreed, viaduct
criss-crossing 116th street fish smells, pinpointing
la marqueta
where elevated trains track over language
run over syllables on elevated tracks, fuse words
together, (w)rap lyrical que pasas on the move
andale, spanglish harlem
nuyorican sidewalks, exploding fried bananas
timbale shopping carts up into salsa
sweat new borinquen slick steps
buzzard winged, moustached, newyorican muchachas
in a new world latin groove, where the truth
of things is what's happening now
the truth of things is what's happening now

# A POEM FOR "MAGIC";

*for Earvin "Magic" Johnson, Donnell Reid and Richard Franklin*


take it to the hoop, "magic" johnson,
take the ball dazzling down the open lane
herk & jerk & raise your six foot nine inch
frame into air sweating screams of your neon name
"magic" Johnson, nicknamed "windex" way back in high school
'cause you wiped glass backboards so clean
where you first juked & shook
& wiled your way to glory
a new styled fusion of shake & bake energy
using everything possible you created your own space
to fly through—any moment now we expect your wings
to spread feathers for that spooky take-off of yours
then shake & glide till you hammer home
a clothesline deuce off glass
now, come back down with a reverse hoodoo gem
off the spin, & stick it in sweet popping nets
clean from twenty feet right side

put the ball on the floor, "magic"
slide the dribble behind your back, ease it deftly
between your bony stork legs, head bobbing everwhichaway
up & down, you see everything on the court, off the high
yoyo patter, stop & go dribble, you shoot
a threading needle rope pass sweet home to kareem
cutting through the lane, his skyhook pops the cords
now lead the fastbreak, hit jamaal on the fly
now blindside a behind the back pinpointpass for two more
off the fake, looking the other way
you raise off balance into tense space
sweating chants of your name, turn 360 degrees
on the move your legs scissoring space like a swimmer's
yo-yoing motion in deep water, stretching out now
towards free flight, you double pump through human trees

hang in place, slip the ball into your left hand
then deal it like a las vegas card dealer off squared glass
into nets living up to your singular nickname, so "bad"
you cartwheel the crowd towards frenzy
wearing now your electric smile, neon as your name

in victory we suddenly sense your glorious uplift
your urgent need to be champion
& so we cheer, rejoicing with you for this quicksilver, quicksilver, quicksilver
moment of fame, so put the ball on the floor again, "magic"
juke & dazzle, shaking & baking down the lane
take the sucker to the hoop, "magic" johnson
recreate reverse hoodoo gems off the spin
deal alley-oop-dunk-a-thon-magician passes, now
double-pump, scissor, vamp through space, hang in place
& put it all in the sucker's face, "magic" Johnson
& deal the roundball like the juju man that you am
like the sho-nuff shaman man that you am
"magic," like the sho-nuff spaceman you am

# LEON THOMAS AT THE TIN PALACE

eye thought it was the music when
in fact it was a blender
grindin down the ice
making stuffings for drinks, but then
you jumped right on in on the downbeat leon
stroking rhythm inside time
inside the bar, then

people flew deeper into themselves
became the very air sweeping language to crescendo
between feathers of touch looping chord changes
your voice blued down, blues cries, field hollas
mississippi river flooded guttural
stitches through your space
images of collective recall, leon

your voicestrokes scattin octaves—
ice grindin down still inside the blender
makin' stuffings for pina coladas—then
you scooped up our feelings again
in the shovel of your john henry doowops, leon
jazzed through ellington count & bird
yodelin' coltrane blues cries
the history of joe williams
sewn into the eyes of our eardrums
transmitted to the space between
the eyes, where memory lies

your scattin licks brings us back dancin'
in our seats, you kick swellin' language inside
your lungs, leon, voice stroking colors paintin'
the Creator's Masterplan
as pharaoh explodes inside the tone blender of his horn

ice grinds down the bar jumps out of itself
scooped up in the shovel of your john henry doowops
blue as a mississippi guttural river flooded
octaves kickin' back black scattin
rhythms loop bustin your chops

feather strokin' phrasin', leon thomas
yodelin' octaves, sewn back black

where they came from

## UNTITLED 3

birds ski down the day's inscrutable smile
wheeling, banking their diaphanous
sawblading voices, their sword-like sleek feathers
cutting through the day's upper reaches of silence
their convoluted language cacophonous
& raucous, as a lynch mob
in old georgia, the rope-rasping burning of their syllables
hanging their twisting meanings around us & these blooming
dark hours stormy with chaos april brings—
spring leaping suddenly upon us
like a black panther clawing our breath
but is filled with so rare & mysterious
a beauty, it thrills us to death

MALE SPRINGTIME RITUAL;
*for Hugh Masekela & Jonathan Blount, eyeballers, each*


it's hard on male eyeballs walking new york streets
in springtime, all the fine flamingo ladies
peeling off everything the cold winter forced them to
put on, now breasts shook loose from strait-jacket overcoats
tease invitations of nipples
peek-a-boo through see through clinging blouses
reveal most things imagination needs to know about
mystery; they jelly-roll, seduce through silk
short-circuit connections of dirty old men
mind in their you-know-what
young men too, fog up eyeglasses, contact lens, shades—
& most of these sho-nuff hope to die, lovers
always get caught without
portable, windex, cleaner bottles
& so have to go blind through the rest of the day
contemplating what they thought they saw

eye mean it can drive you crazy walking behind one of those
memorable asses, in springtime, when the wind gets cocky
& licks up one of those breeze-blown, slit, wraparounds, revealing
that grade A sweet rump of flesh is moving like those old black
african ladies taught it to do & do
eye mean, it's maybe too much
for a good old, staid, episcopal, christian chauvinist
with a bad heart & a pacer
eye mean, what can we expect him to do—
carrying that kind of heavy baggage around—
but vote for bras to be worn everyday
& abolish any cocky wind whose tongue gets completely out
of hand, liftin up skirts of fine, young, sweet thangs
eye mean, there ought to be a law against some things
eye'm sure he would say, "reckless eyeballin"
eye'm sure he would say

anyway, its hard on us menfolk streetwalkers in springtime
liable too find your eyeballs roaming around dazed
in some filthy new york city gutter
knocked there by some dazzling beauty who happened along
your field of vision—who knows, next thing you know
they'll be making pacers for eyeballs—
who cares if you go down for the whole ten count
& never pull your act back together again, & so become
a bowery street, babbling idiot, going on & on
about some fine, flamingo lady you thought
you saw, an invitation, perhaps
who cares if her teasing breasts shook you
everwhichaway but loose

it's springtime in the old big apple
& all the fine flamingo ladies are peeling off
everything the cold forced them to put on
their breasts shake loose from overcoats
tease invitations of nipples
it's all a part of the springtime ritual

& only the strongest eyeballs, survive

# EYE THROW MY ROPE TONGUE INTO THE SKY

eye throw my rope tongue into the sky
send words of love lassoing to you cross
blue valleys of distance
fight off midwestern tornados, desert fried
fools who want to intercept this message for you
only for you, rain-swept cooing lady wooing
tongue of cool rain
my voice, a wing of soothing feathers
riffing & riding the hot wires, comes tickling
your eardrums, my sweet tongue looping
lyrical melodies of fire
rope tongue looping melodies cross skies
comes tickling, sweetly, your eardrums

## A THOUGHT FOR YOU, MARGARET
*for Margaret Porter*


eye stretch my lips, 3000 miles
cross telephone wires, sucking silence
of wings beating down breath, space
a hemorrhage of distance

& you there singing, as dusktones
rainbow feathers, sleeping, as loveliness
peace, we have come to this magic, apart
with ourselves, alone
serene, inside this music

muted trumpet kissing fabled dusk song
skin of scarred history, long distant embraces
in dreams, memory easing out of breath, rhythms
gliding, in & out, over & under
like birds—footprints in white snow—
banking down sunset skies

& now your love call coming through
clear, the night wind's sucking deep mystery
through space, black distance collapsing in
on itself, screaming, the grip
of your sonorous, name

soothing, tongue touch, your sonorous name

# A POEM FOR OJENKE & K. CURTIS LYLE

if in a comatose instant of deep listening
you should come across a syllable
wide as the sky of pure hearing & steep
as wherever anytime your eyes carry themselves
to their limits of recognition, crystal
as on a steel blue day of bright clear winter
at the moment of that rare clarity
as in the listening to a black blues band there
steeped in the bone & blood utterance of gut-bucket
bucket of blood tradition, if in the stop-action
freezing of that negative
snapped image heard & fashioned there
from that sound you just perceived now in the knowing
of that terror, just now, there, guttural
as in the whiskey-broken voice life of ma rainey
chained to microscopic grooving of a vinyl instance
recorded then full of all things considered
meaningful there—then, as now—
what it all means when everything is left
hanging out there in the cold, like blood-spattered
sheets billowing under a lolling blue morning
cool rinse that now switches up
under a chameleon sun's heat, now, like cynical
laughter, sweating down rivers of gold light
beamed there, & if in the rifle sighting
focusing of that clearly cold instant
comatosed, you should happen across a syllable
wide as the sky of new hearing & blue deep
blue deep, as where anytime your vision carries
itself to limits of recognition
if you should hear a crystal song ringing out
there, & during that moment of rare clarity
a voice, perhaps, a note like a breeze fluting over
informing this moment, perhaps, a cool blue morning

rinsed, folding over a beginning poem there
& in the crystal clear hearing of that moment
& in the bone & blood spirit of gut-bucket blues
tradition, you should hear a new crystal image
there, call me with a poem, good brothers
call me & singing, call me through a poem

# SOUTHERN LYRIC; RITUAL

evenings rise here with voices of old people
whispering up sky, a cat-eyed moon riding
wings of bat syllables rising
brushing up against mystery, eyelids of language
winking their hushing rhythms through serenading trees
xylophones carrying cooling winds to memory
couch their soothing sounds in magic of primeval wisdom
the orchestration of harmony between ensembles of birds
whose voices whisper riffings up steep skies
carrying history a lynx-eyed moon rides up on
rising, like muted tongues of old people
ventriloquists of southern nights
whispering there on porches
cobwebbed in filigreed shadows
half light, the old peoples' voices
yeasting with wisdom in their sundown
eyes, riding up sky, longside a lynx-
eyed moon, wings of bat syllables
soothing, a xylophone, a tune

CONJURING AGAINST ALIEN SPIRITS;
*for Ishmael Reed*


if there is something that takes you
to the brink of terror
turn your pockets inside out, like a lolling dog's
tongue, salivating, in heat, make a screech-
owl's death cry go away, go away
make a screech-owl's death
cry go away, go away

turn shoes upside down at your own
front door, tie a knot in your apron string mama
sister, throw fire on salt
talk to raw head & bloody bones
make a hoot owl screaming death
go home, take it away
make a hoot owl take it away on home

turn your pillow inside out
see a cross-eyed devilish-fool, cross
your fingers—drop gooberdust in your mind medicine
eat a root doctor's magic root—spit on them
make a cross in the road
where you met yourself going
& coming, spit on it

that same spot where you passed over
in the road, spit on it, to soften up enemies
walk backwards along any road you passed over
before, red moon, like a one-eyed
wino's stare, stuck in bone
shadowed trees, throw dirt over
your left shoulder, spit down on it
in the road, on that same spot where your terror
locked itself into another enigma

where someone's footprints leave their signatures
of weight, define shapes of worn soles
speak to raw head & bloody bones
great-great-great grandmama
make a hoot owl screaming death

take his case all the way home
screaming, all the way home
make a hoot owl screaming death

take your death slip all the way home

## PASSING ON THE LEGACY;
*for my son, Brandon Troupe & Henry Dumas*


we stand within these bones
of ourselves within
flesh of these years melting
as ice cubes in drinks
within stone these thoughts
this miracle of roots inside
our folklore the link
stretching four hundred years
back to villages eaten black
by euro-american halloween flames
eating up the dark rhythms rhythms
eating up the dark rhythms rhythms

here weaving shadows dance
through leaves stretch to hear
across salt water the bugaman high
in trees the drummers harden hands

& time breaks wind & bone
stone juxtaposed next to feathers

& there aren't too many secrets
these days that are not known we speak
through our eyes
& see through our ears & hear
through our tongues

we stand within tone of these bones
inside these years ringing like bells
a coltrane solo solo
& so eye reach out the smile
of my tongue blue-black with blues rhythms
a jazz-riff born of dues payments

to you a love gong
chiming from my eyes
hand over to you this signature
born in blood & fire
& baptized in river-bottoms

a sun-toned hardness
a guitar full of lives

so take the vision brandon
& run up sun with it
look back into your eyes

you are the memory
carrying the future

# NEW YORK CITY STREAM POEM

sounds    sounds of crushed traffic
winds sounds    sounds
symphonic voices of multi-lingual people
of new york city people    moving
through space    pace
of kinetic energy
                       energy of space/place

of new york city space/place
a pickpocket of energy new york giving energy
                                city space/place
space/place of music    colors
energy of music    colors    & sounds weaving motion
rhythm guitar dancers of sound
                       motion

& faces    odd cold beautiful faces
& legs & figures that burst out of colors
races
traces of races that move beyond races    colors that
fuse & blues the only language we know hear
faces sensuous faces
faces with lips that invite    sounds
they are succulent
they are very very succulent
these sounds    these colors
these lips that invite

colors    traces of races
in the fused shadow world leaping
from faces    lips that invite
sounds    colors of sound
color me sound color me motion color me
wind sound motion

                    color me poem
color me African wind poem
color me music
color me African freedom music
                    color me black

color me traces of races
bursting from colors moving beyond races
color me faces    sensuous faces
lips that invite
                    color me energy
color me voodoo/hoodoo
space/place of energy
color me motion moving

color me love color me love
color me hoodoo/voodoo
traces of races in love

color me love

## AT THE END

at the end
of every sentence
a period
occupying space
as molecular energy

a point to make
another point
in space the end is
the beginning
of another end

recurring cycles
occupying space

& death being
only a period at the
end of a sentence

earth

a point
that starts
another point

& at the end
there is space
to begin again

always space
at the end to
begin again

5

---

FROM WEATHER REPORTS, 1991

# PERENNIAL RITUAL
*for all the dictators of Haiti & anywhere else*


they are killing the joy of laughter once again
they're slaughtering the smiles of children
they're banning the music from language once again
they're marching in goose-steps to rhythm of bullets
they're putting cyanide in people's drinks of hope again
they're trading back their freedom for strings of puppet money
they're digging mass graves for the innocent once more
they're cutting down trees that hold back the floods
they're macheteing roots of their bloodlines once again
they're smearing blood on their mother's faces dead as moats
they're ripping out the tongues from their history again
they're butchering all love like they would a goat

what is it that they hate in themselves, in clear, new mirrors
what is the dry as bone spit of their snake-eyed fear, their terror
of bloodlines, running deep as the secrets of voodoo
what is the future they want everyone to dance through
where did the poison come from that is flowing through their puffer-fish
hearts & where do their thoughts turn to after uzis shoot joy from the dark
& the eerie silent roads hold only the shadows of murderers

bufo marinus namphy, sweating beneath his tunics medalled with skulls
his henchmen sitting black stone-faced behind him with their slit cobra eyes
cool & evil prosper avril & william regala, lafontant & old bossman, duvalier
what is the suicidal urge they pick up from other scumbags
licking out their lizard tongues cancerous with warts
their dum-dum, bazooka eyes of mamba snakes
deadly as a fart at a republican party, whose American president keeps them
stumbling here with his famous soft shoe, his chicken neck flapping clues
his glued hair plastered in place, embodying what they will sink to
what they will kill for to become
O, they're shooting out the lights of port-au-prince once again
they're turning people into zombies with their snake-eye guns

{ *173* }

they're trying to kill the moon in a dreamer's eyes once more
they're feeding the vacant-eyed poor with teaspoons half-filled with garbage
they're lining up beggars & killing their hunger again
they are goose-stepping to the rhythm of bullets

# BOOMERANG: A BLATANTLY POLITICAL POEM

eye use to write poems about burning
down the motherfucking country for crazy
horse, geronimo & malcolm king
x, use to (w)rite about stabbing white folks
in their air-conditioned eyeballs with ice picks
cracking their sagging balls with sledgehammer blows
now, poems leap from the snake-tip of my tongue
bluesing a language twisted tighter than braided hope
hanging like a limp-noosed rope down the question mark
back of some coal miner's squaw, her razor slanted
killer shark eyes swollen shut with taboos
she thought she heard & knew
the sun in a voice looking like bessie smith's severed arm
on that mississippi back road, screaming, like a dead man's son
who had to watch his old man eat his own pleading heart
& sometimes eye wonder if it's worth the bother
of it all, these poems eye (w)rite holding
language percolating & shaped
into metaphoric rage
underneath, say
a gentle simile, like a warm
spring day, soft as balm or talcum
on the edge of a tornado that hits quicker
than the flick of a bat's wing nicking the eye
eye use to write poems about killing fools like ronald reagan
daffy duck grinning off 30 million sucked down
the whirlpooling black holes of cia space
director casey taking a lobotomy
hit, slash to protect
the gipper
dumb
motherfuckers
everywhere tying bombs

to their own tongues, lighting fuses
of staged events that lye of peace & saving
money in the s & l pirateering, like president gipper
they are metaphors for all that's wrong in america right now, all this
cloning, brouhaha, paid mouthpieces on wall street & the gipper
giving frying skillet speeches, others that ray gun reagan
ray gunning america, now, cannibalizing airwaves
with mouthpieces fronting slimy churches
building up humongous bank accounts
in the name of the holy bones
of jesus christ, long gone
& dead
& it is a metaphor
boomeranging jimmy
& tammy baker, sleazy swaggert
vacuuming pocketbooks of the old & the dead
like medusa meese heads nicked off & sluicing like bad faith
they dangle heads from "freedom fighter" mouths
tell the black bird press herded up on a wire
that it's okay, it's okay, it's okay
& them believing it
eye use to write poems about burning
down the motherfucking country for crazy
horse, geronimo & malcolm king
x marks the spot where "coons" signed away
their lives on dotted lines, black holes
sucking away their breath
for a sack of cotton
full of woe
eye
sit here
now, (w)riting
poems of the soft
calm beauty welling
in my son's innocent 4 year
old eyes, thinking, perhaps of the time

when this rage will strike him, driving him towards madness
knowing all the while it will come quick
sooner than expected
& nothing
absolutely nothing
will have been undone

# LES CAYES, HAITI & RELIGIONS
# ON PARADE: 1984

### 1. VOODOO
on good Friday, fronting the square
rara called the few old faithful here through
bamboo, the drum masters stroking their signatures
rooted clues deep beneath the surface, voodoo
found its medium in lulu
the lithe, loa dancer
baton twirlers, beyond the blues
that lightning spoke in a mojo hand
a mojo hand, a sequined loa called through
sluicing, bamboo clues, voice deep
in voodoo, a mojo hand, calling
somewhere, somehow, old
lightning hopkins knew
came close to playing
what this was all about

### 2. CATHOLICISM
the catholic parade hustled many through
droves moved through the dark streets of les cayes
mixed bloods & pure bloods walking shoulder to shoulder
the crucifiction myth nailed in all their heads
nailed in their hearts, bloods
bearing up the cross through the dark
the hymns of jesus christ's blood running
through their voices up ahead, pulling
blood of three nails hammered down
through centuries of His blood
running like ribbons through these streets
reining ropes pulling His invisible image, here
through these litanies of blood
& bloody all these bodies snaking through
les cayes, full of nails driven through

open palms & feet, screaming
their bloody, burdened, invisible voices
of mythical blood flowing invisible through
these dark, narrow streets
the many faithful meet, shoulder to shoulder
mixed bloods & pure bloods, carrying
their crosses in their voices
shoulder to shoulder, snaking through les cayes
les cayes, spirit to spirit, on this good Friday
evening & all of them deep in voodoo, too

3.  THE PROTESTANTS
the protestants were silent on this day
& perhaps their silence spoke for them, too
whatever their numbers
silence spoke this evening for them, too
who were not there

## IN JIMMY'S GARDEN
*for James Baldwin (1924–1987)*


this sunday morning breaks blue clear, in st paul de vence
the november dew glazing green grass, luminous, here
where the crowned soul of sunlight slants beamed glances of gold
across & over the gabled, slate, 300 year old rooftop of the gentle black
man, sleeping here, swallowed up by a mackintosh shirt, that is a tent
wrapped around his vanishing body, his mind still alert & beautiful
as this bird, singing valley, in southern france
where eye hear, now, a dog barking deep in the muffled distance
where tire wheels spin & wear their licking, rubber speech, mimicking wind
voices spinning themselves, in a constant rush, over asphalt, brush my ears
here, like gushing sounds of sea & sand ground up
into crushed dreams, whispering for the listener

& here & now & under this canopied trellis of grape leaves
in summer gone frost brown & yellow now with coming winter
eye focus my poet's camera, through this pen eye am using now & see
these hills, wrapping themselves, like legs of a sensuous woman around
this poem, like similar valleys & mountains in haiti
& so eye transport myself here & now over 5000 miles to that place
tortured with hunger, sudden death, voodoo & wafting smoke
curling up sea-green valleys—like here—stinging nostrils
& ask for the hougon's help in delivering this deep sleeping
wordsmith, shrinking up under the slate, gabled roof
chewing, invisible, piranha teeth, tearing away his flesh

& here & now, in this early breaking, sun-blue, moment, he is
moving past it all, in deep knowing, to a peaceful place
beyond this sweet, adopted space of torture, miraculous with glory
the poetry of birds & the sea sound of wheels fusing their speech
mimicking wind voices licking rubber over asphalt
& he is moving beyond all of us, now, even his brother's voice
breaking low, in his bedroom & mingling with a former lover's murmur
raising in the 300 year old farmhouse, like the new coffee brewing

in the pot, in this new day & we will be warmed by the croissants
heating in the ancient oven, where the old smiling french woman
is bent over, now, while above my aging head
brown shrivelled grapes, die on the vine—
prisoners of time & fate—like you
O great wordsmith—"mouth on paper of the revolution"—
your spirit, now, moving beyond even the wings of night

your spirit, now, moving & fusing, with the light

IN MEMORIAM

*for James Baldwin (1924–1987)*


it's like a gray, dreary day, wet with tears & mourning
when someone you love ups & goes away
leaving behind a hole in your laughter, an empty space
following you around, like an echo you always hear & never see
high up in the mountains
the spirit gone & left, circling, there, its diminishing sound
a song looking for a place inside this gray day of tears
to lay down its earthly load
to drop down its weary voice among the many blue ones missing
there, who are elbowing their clacking bones, rattling, like false teeth
loose in a jelly jar, up against each other, their voices
dead as lead, & silence yawning
with the indifference final breaths achieve
& the open mouths are black holes framing endless space
words fall through, like stars sprinkled through the breath
of your holy sentences, jimmy
up there now with the glorious voices of bessie
the glory hallelujah, shouting gospel
you loved so deeply, wrote it out in your blood
running like dazzling rivers of volcanic lava, blood
so dazzling, your words blooming van gogh sunflowers
you planted, as sacred breaths inside our minds & hearts
the image of the real deal going down funky & hard

& so we celebrate you, holy witness, celebrate
your skybreaking smile, infectious laughter
hear your glory hallelujah warnings everywhere we look
see clearly, the all-american, scrubbed down, button down
greed, rampant, in these "yet to be united states"
& so we take heed, beg for your forgiveness, that you might
forgive us for our smallness, for not rising up with you
for being less than our awesome, pitiful needs

forgive us now in your silence, jimmy
forgive us all who knew & were silent & fearful
& forgive us all, O wordsaint, who never even listened
forgive us for all the torture, for all the pain

## AVALANCHE AFTERMATH

*for Earl Maxie*

outside lake tahoe, we see, scorched, white bones
of stake-like trees, felled (they remind of crude war
weapons, sharpened & hidden & pointing up from pits)
cutting a wide path through murmuring, green
pines, pointing their branches, accusingly up, at a steel blue
spring sky, crystal clear above our voices, where the highway once
loped & looped back, winding down from echo summit
the year before half the mountain walked clean across the american river
intact, to the other side of the road, thrown there after an avalanche
triggered abrupt & permanent change in the way things were
like a track of train rails, switching up directions, after
the juice is thrown at the main, power station: & it reminds
us, that destinations are always in the hands of God

# PORTER, AT 18 MONTHS

*for Porter Troupe*

you slipped down into this world, porter
during the dead hours of night
slipped down in a form already perfect, kicking
a screaming bursting from your new, ballooning lungs
older than time, though young in this miraculous
moment of celebration
& you were the mysterious, meaning of magic, porter
the fused dialectic of passion, alchemized
a sweet miracle, beyond all words

& now, already, you speak in a strange tongue
to birds & ants
           & now, already, you terrorize the cat
from his sun-nap, & draw your exploding imagination
over all the clean walls
           & now, already, you reject
with disdain, all helping hands
& go about your business in your own way

full of wonder, we watch you grow into yourself
filling out your own imagination, charting your own course
like an explorer, discovering new worlds
opening up before you, like flowers

& we are both amazed & afraid, knowing the way
in front of you will be treacherously beautiful
having travelled this road, before

so now, we teach you bonding principles, absent of miracles
but soon—very soon—we will stand aside & let you go

CHANGE
*for Margaret & Porter*


use to be eye would be lying there
in margaret's lap, longside her sweet
soft thighs, on Sunday mornings, sipping
champagne, sucking on her soft, open lips
drinking in the love from her moist, brown eyes
now, porter's there, giggling, twenty month old
squirming squeals—a tiny, spitting image of me—
his eyes kissing everyone, including me, & me?
well, eye'm sitting here, apart from them
hungry, alone, in my favorite chair
watching television & listening to them
& watching them, watching me

# SIMPLE JOYS

my young son, porter, watching snowflakes
whoops, in ecstasy, as they collect, like lint
on the front windshield of my car, his growing
hands try to snag them through the tinted glass
as they hit & melt, like dead faces time erases
in a flash, though he misses & leaves only his
handprints on the tinted glass, there, his sudden
simple joy of discovering, suddenly, switching
like the attention span of television
his eyes now locked onto spinning, car wheels
churning in surprise, his imagination scotchtaping
itself to everything, tripping over everything, turning
snowflakes into flowers, brown brushstrokes stroking
the windshield become the tail of our cat, tchikaya
window bars, baseball bats in the eyes of his dazzling
invention, wonder residing there, like magic
everyday the curtain going up on his transforming
pure eyes, that see metaphors everywhere
& it gives me sweet joy in this age of cynicism
to watch & be with him, tripping through discovery—
his simple joys the envy of my caged wisdom

## EYE WALK

eye walk, liquid footsteps of my words
across tongue bridge, to where you stand
just now, offer you these bittersweet syllables
pregnant with history of what
we have seen together, metaphors,
as in the color of sea breezes & wind, rustling
hairdos of trees, tossing & turning in the ebb & flow
of meaning between us, the rhythms of your seduction
flowing into sound of your body breathing
just outside, now, my ears, where your licking
tongue—a breeze, blowing softly—teases
your voice, a mere whisper & your pouting lips
shaping a kiss, succulent, as a plum, bursting

## TOUT DE MÊME——NICE & MALIBU

the cote d'azur
like the coast of malibu—
a necklace of lights

# 21 LINES TO CARNOT, GUADELOUPIAN MASTER DRUMMER

his wood & zinc house hard by the bay in goyave
carnot, master of traditional, guadeloupian, le woz
drumming, six other palm to skin, rhythms, he of the flying
hands, cracking thunder, he splits the silent speech of night
machete fingers cleaving a passageway
voices flowing through ancestral
cadences, pulsating lyrical, voodoo, sewing breezes
painting pastel music, from deep inside itself
a secret language swells the way to magic, ritual
whose ears have heard the mystery of love, unfolding

holding the history of doves, a sea crab scuttles over
the stone floor, cold & hard, as poverty, carnot leans, strong
his body, an exclamation mark—
& sharp as a honed, sword's blade, the edges torn & jagged
as starpoints screwed into his peasant, catfish eyes
the electric boring up deep simmering coals, burning from within
the steady gaze, hawk-like, holds the sky
cruising through his two, brown lagoons—
leans into the sea, salted wind, where he goes
a fisherman, drumming, his life, the last of his kind here—

african roots dropping secret notes from his palms

## POEM FOR MY FATHER

*for Quincy T. Trouppe Sr.*


father, it was an honor to be there, in the dugout
with you, the glory of great black men swinging their lives
as bats, at tiny white balls
burning in at unbelievable speeds, riding up & in & out
a curve breaking down wicked, like a ball falling off a table
moving away, snaking down, screwing its stitched magic
into chitlin circuit air, its comma seams spinning
toward breakdown, dipping, like a hipster
bebopping a knee-dip stride, in the charlie parker forties
wrist curling, like a swan's neck
behind a slick black back
cupping an invisible ball of dreams

& you there, father, regal, as an african, obeah man
sculpted out of wood, from a sacred tree, of no name, no place, origin
thick branches branching down, into cherokee & someplace else lost
way back in africa, the sap running dry
crossing from north carolina into georgia, inside grandmother mary's
womb, where your mother had you in the violence of that red soil
ink blotter news, gone now, into blood graves
of american blues, sponging rococo
truth long gone as dinosaurs
the agent-oranged landscape of former names
absent of african polysyllables, dry husk, consonants there
now, in their place, names, flat, as polluted rivers
& that guitar string smile always snaking across
some virulent, american, redneck's face
scorching, like atomic heat, mushrooming over nagasaki
& hiroshima, the fever blistered shadows of it all
inked, as etchings, into sizzled concrete
but you, there, father, through it all, a yardbird solo
riffing on bat & ball glory, breaking down the fabricated myths
of white major league legends, of who was better than who

beating them at their own crap
game, with killer bats, as bud powell swung his silence into beauty
of a josh gibson home run, skittering across piano keys of bleachers
shattering all manufactured legends up there in lights
struck out white knights, on the risky edge of amazement
awe, the miraculous truth sluicing through
steeped & disguised in the blues
confluencing, like the point at the cross
when a fastball hides itself up in a slider, curve
breaking down & away in a wicked, sly grin
curved & posed as an ass-scratching uncle tom, who
like old sachel paige delivering his famed hesitation pitch
before coming back with a hard, high, fast one, is slicker
sliding, & quicker than a professional hitman—
the deadliness of it all, the sudden strike
like that of the "brown bomber's" crossing right
of sugar ray robinson's, lightning, cobra bite

& you, there, father, through it all, catching rhythms
of chono pozo balls, drumming, like conga beats into your catcher's mitt
hard & fast as "cool papa" bell jumping into bed
before the lights went out

of the old, negro baseball league, a promise, you were
father, a harbinger, of shock waves, soon come

## POEM FOR THE ROOT DOCTOR OF ROCK N ROLL
*for Chuck Berry*

& it all came together on the mississippi river
chuck, you there riding the rocking-blue sound wave
duck-walking the poetry of hoodoo down
        & you were the mojo-hand
of juju crowing, the gut-bucket news—running it down
for two records sold to make a penny
back then in those first days, "majoring in mouth"—
a long, gone, lean lightning rod
      picking the edge, charging the wires
        of songs, huckle-bucking "roll over
beethoven," playing "devil's music," till white devils stole it from you
& called it their own, "rock n roll"
        devils like elvis & pat boone
who never duck-walked back in the alley with you
& bo diddley, little richard & the fatman from new orleans
all yall slapping down songs meaner than the smell
of toejam & rot-gut whiskey breath
back there, in them back rooms
      of throw down


back there, here your song lyrics grew, like fresh corn
you, chuck berry, an authentic american genius of barbecue sauce
& deep fried catfish licks, jack-salmon guitar
       honky-tonk rhythms
jangling warm, vibrating sounds, choo-chooing train
whistles fiddling & smoking down the tracks of the blues
motivating through "little queenie," "maybelline"
decked out in red on sarah & finney
alarms rolling off your whipping tongue
in the words of "johnny b good"
you clued us in, back to the magical hookup of ancestors
their seamless souls threading your breath
     their blood in your sluicing strut

& too much "monkey business," the reason for their deaths, cold & searing
your spirit reaching down to the bones of your roots
deep in the "show me" blood of missouri soil
                                        your pruned, hawk-look, profiling
where you rode your white cadillac of words, cruising
the highways of language (what we speak & hear even now)
breathing inside your cadences
                            you shaped & wheeled the music
duck-walking the length of the stage
duck-walked your zinging metaphors of everyday
slip-slide & strut, vibrating your hummingbird wings
your strumming style, the cutting edge
you were what was to come


so hail, hail, chuck berry, root doctor of "rock n roll"
authentic american genius
                                tonguing deep in river syllables
hail, hail, chuck berry, laying down the motivating juju
you great, american, mojo hand


root doctor, spirit, of american, "rock n roll"

# REFLECTIONS ON GROWING OLDER

eye sit here, now, inside my fast thickening breath
the whites of my catfish eyes, muddy with drink
my roped, rasta hair snaking down in twisted salt & pepper
vines braided from the march of years, pen & ink lines etching
my swollen face, the collected weight of years swelling
around my middle, the fear of it all overloading circuits
here & now with the weariness of tears, coming on in storms
the bounce drained out of my once liquid strut
a stork-like gimpiness there now, stiff as death
my legs climbing steep stairs in protest now, the power gone
slack from when eye once heliocoptered through cheers, hung around rims
threaded rainbowing jumpshots, that ripped, popped cords & envious peers
gone, now the cockiness of that young, firm flesh
perfect as arrogance & the belief that perpetual hard-ons would swell
forever here, smoldering fire in a gristle's desire, drooping limp now
like wet spaghetti, or noodles, the hammer-head that once shot straight in
& ramrod hard into the sucking sweet heat of wondrous women
wears a lugubrious melancholy now, like an old frog wears its knobby head
croaking like a lonely malcontent through midnight hours
eye sit here, now, inside my own gathering flesh
thickening into an image of humpty-dumpty
at the edge of a fall, the white of my hubris gone
muddy as mississippi river water
eye feel now the assault of shotgunned years
shortening breath, charlie horses throbbing through cold
tired muscles, slack & loose as frayed, old ropes
slipping from round the neck of an executed memory
see, now, these signals of irreversible breakdowns—
the ruination of my once, perfect flesh—as medals earned
fighting through the holy wars of passage, see them as miracles
of the glory of living breath, pulsating music through my poetry—
syncopating metaphors turned here inside out—
see it all now as the paths taken, the choices made
the loves lost & broken, the loves retained
& the poems lost & found in the dark
beating like drumbeats through the heart

# FALLING DOWN ROADS OF SLEEP

we are falling down roads into sleep
falling into sleep from blues
posing as the sky, the eye of the Creator, moves
black cataracts of clouds around, pointillistic, as clues
wet, as when a bad knee tells us that rain is coming
before night floods down the streets
sleep is seducing, as the light
slips from the night, slips from our eyes
& slides across the sky, like feet over ice
the lances of our intentions, glancing off moons
slicing the edge of noon
we remember a sky blue & deep with light
remember the wings of birds turning around hours
burning off suns, flights of music diving toward night
like warring elements, our speech thunderclapping
down streets lugubrious with sleep
deep down we leap, back into sleep, so steep
the fall back into blues
we forget the fading of night, coming
begin climbing up ladders of song, rung by rung
sleep falling between our language, now, lifting
toward flight, rain clouds, like circling crows
cruise under light, under the bold
gold polished coin of the sun, holding

# UNTITLED

in brussels, eye sat in the grand place cafe & heard
duke's place, played after salsa
between the old majestic architecture, jazz bouncing off
all that gilded gold history snoring complacently there
flowers all over the ground, up inside the sound
the old white band jamming the music
tight & heavy, like some food
pushin pedal to the metal
getting all the way down
under the scaffolding surrounding
l'hotel de ville, chattanooga choochoo
choo chooing all the way home, upside walls, under gold eagles
& a gold vaulting girl, naked on a rooftop holding a flag over
her head, like skip rope, surrounded by all manner
of saints & gold madmen, riding emblazoned stallions
snorting like crazed demons at their nostrils
the music swirling like a dancing bear
a beautiful girl, flowers in her hair

the air woven with lilting voices in this grand place of parapets
& crowns, jewels & golden torches streaming
like a horse's mane, antiquity riding through in a wheel carriage
here, through gargoyles & gothic towers rocketing swordfish lanced crosses
pointing up at a God threatening rain
& it is stunning at this moment when raised beer steins cheer
the music on, hot & heavy, still humming & cooking
basic african-american rhythms alive here
in this ancient grand place of europe
this confluence point of nations & cultures
jumping off place for beer & cuisines
fused with music, poetry & stone
here in this blinding, beautiful square
sunlit now as the golden eye of God shoots through
flowers all over the cobbled ground, up in the music
the air brightly cool as light after jeweled rain

## FOLLOWING THE NORTH STAR BOOGALOO
*for Miguel Algarin*

following the north star boogaloo
the rhythm takes me
back to where music began
to percolate language like coffee in another form
back before frederick douglass laid it down
heavy on abe lincoln
when music was breakdancing, old hottentots
throwing down mean as bojangles ever did
now jump forward through history's dice game
pick up the steps of james brown
michael jackson moonwalking
the old blues talking about yo mama
now fast forward down the lane
pick up the dance of 5 brothers
skateboarding the court
out in the open, one closes the break
after taking it to the hole off the coast to coast
doing a 180 degree phi slamma jamma dunk
before they all high five & glad hand after
stamping their footprints all up in the paint
up in this poet's word dribble
a drummer's paradiddle
word up, yo bro, hip hop, rappers
skateboarding the go go out in the open
court of macking the holy ghost down

hey you, diddle-diddle, voodoo griot, take me
back to when eye was black & hitting proud
out on the slick bop thoroughfares
back before the mean homeboys rolled snarling
duckwaddle down the middle, eyes empty with death
before the alley-oops wore their lives as chips on shoulders
in stratospheric attitudes, hung dip from wall to wall

chained gold, cap bills on heads quaking sideways
muscling up bold masterblasters
checking out reeboks
chillin dead up in the cut "fresh" as "death"
after "mo money," "mo money," "mo money"
check it out bro, pharmaceutical wizards
making 7 figure bank accounts do somersaults, no sweat
it's rolling in so fast for crack ("& it ain't nothing
but a hole in the wall") for homeboys
cash n carry, cold 16 year olds
who cant count nothing  but greenbacks
sliding off the screen & roll, they helicopter
after dipping & rolling down the middle
high up above the paint, their footprints walking on space
up over your face hang gliding to the basket, like praying mantises
so fresh they make pootbutts faint slamming
faster than high fiving glory—
180 degrees of schoolboy legends, saints
unfolding in prime time memory

so roll it back, kojak, before magic's knees go permanently
south for the winter, & leave air jordan's footprints
in yo face game as the baddest one in town
before they change up the shake & bake, jam off the sky again with a new
phenom double clutching up there in space, like a ferrari stretching out
flat out burning up german autobahns, changing up the guard quicker
than fear brings down doodoo
but hey, young bro, flash the dice roll back through shit
to when the big O was jackknifing through all them bodies
out on the court, to when goose tatum was shimmying magic
down in the middle, down in the paint
as roy haynes jitterbugged like a magician
hoola hoopin' the ball around him, before fast forwarding to dr. j
　　—Julius Erving!
& did we ever think we'd lose the hoodoo gods
to old age homes for roundball royalty
new age homeboys not even knowing who they are

& do they even know about jonestown, all them
bloated bodies cracking beneath the sun
& did they ever hear about the north carolina
astronaut, david skywalking thompson
jamming out in the open, off the fly
helicoptering to roundball heaven
off the motherfucking coast to coast
before he took the fall for all that shit
he snorted up his nose, before hitting the pipe
that took him right on out like a blown lightbulb—
way back before kenny anderson was even
a glint in his parents pick n roll eyes

before he skateboarded off the juju fake
picked up his dribble, like magic
then rose up in space like hallelujah 4th of july
glory, before dropping a deuce or a trey quick
as a pickpocket off the slide by
sleight of hand trick, eased on by like mojo with his yoyo
pitter patter, now you see me, now you don't, yo bro
whodunit, poor guy got caught in kenny's schoolyard
voodoo, jump back in the alley
say what? did you see that motherfucking bad-boy sky?
past where it all started, somewhere back before
language followed the north star boogaloo
dancing back when they was hamboning the black
bottom for fun, back then in the language
when homeboys picked cotton
played the dozens; "eye hate to talk about yo mama
she was a good old soul, but she got a two-ton pussy
& an iron ass hole, & yo daddy got a dick
big as a motherfucking toothpick!"

say what chu say, say what chu say? say what?

word, when we knew ourselves through songs
through what we saw alive in homeboys eyes

through love, through what it was we were before
commercials told us how to move & groove, who to love
when we did it all & had fun & knew the heroes
new & old & never confused dope for the bomb
back before we fast forwarded to integration
entered the 60s on a bullshit tip
lost ourselves in the fast forwarding
70s & 80s, in the cloning xerox machines
before kenny anderson skateboarded
his prince of a hip hop, roundball game
breakrapping all the way to roundball legend

up north, south of the voodoo connection
north of where we entered from africa

# 6

---

FROM AVALANCHE, 1996

# THE SOUND, BREAKING AWAY

finger touching breeze there gentle in air    almost silent
save voices of birds    winging in midair banking
down & over mountains
                                                    when suddenly there is
movement in the craning upward of necks of animals
startled glances pop fear around & around
suddenly
                                    above it all is the beginning of a sound
crip   crip   carip   crip
                                crip   crip   carip   crip
crip   crip   carip   crip   crip   carip   crack   crak   carip


crack


the sound in crevices under rock high up in the mountains
the sound now in the air is of a pulling away
a crack in the plate of rock breaking


                            caaa-rack   crack   caaa-rack
                                crack   crack   caaa-rack   crack
                                                    caaa-rack


the assonance of sound breaking from ground
breaking away from itself & found in the bounding syllables of snow
moving now            beginning to roar above the cracking
                                                    separation
            crack   crack   caaa-racking   rocks   breaking


away from themselves   a movement   as if raising rock
hands skyward in prayer toward the creator
& is a breaking away of syllables   a breaking & tumbling & shattering
            language flaking
off verbs shaking off original meaning & swirling in a white storm
            of words that resemble
snowflakes roaring down a mountain

of words mounting other words creating their own wind
storms of flatted fifths & drumrolls snarling down & around & around
& the maelstrom is a piranha of sound eating up ears with verbs
sounds building into a blizzard of metaphors spread around & around
as eyes spread wide in disbelief as words rain down
in hurricane fury      up inside a giant snowball of verbs
rocks & severed arms & tree limbs
pinwheeling & rolling    in a boiling white statement of adjectives & nouns

& the verbs   voom   vooming   galoom   galoom voodun galoom
          galoom voom vooming   galoom galoom galoom doom doom

& then it's over suddenly as it began

only clouds of white words swirl around the new eddying
white doves swirling up in cold air
as if they were white lace floating skyward torn off wedding dresses
cold as snow crystals here   the air prickling
the once shattering roar quiet
now above the whispering

wind

& the birds   mute witnesses   gliding into view
as new life settles   after verbs blew
the color of snow as metaphor through this poem—
the theme of renewal evoked—
as winter becomes spring becomes
summer becomes autumn
becomes ad infinitum
in continuous cycles of seeding
growing & mending
breaking away   everywhere

as avalanches of sound
& words create new language

everywhere

# WATCH OUT FOR SOUND BITES & SPIN DOCTORS

the silliness of it all rushing like cartoons through black holes drilled
inside our heads & once there became instant throwaway images
wrapped in plastic, like our hunger for fast foods & zippered smiles
glued to faces blow-dried hair politicians wear decked out in shiny
suits everywhere, their hands all wet & clammy with bile
greed & indifference, spinning their sordid messages through sound bites
as they puppet-doll dance through sold air strung up flashing snake eyes
pulsating images of bulging gold nuggets, watch out as they bore openings
into our heads, pore themselves sporting wire-attached halos
the wind all funky hot around them, as television cameras—hand operated
from shoulders of men scurrying around like roaches apprehended
in broad daylight—glint their buglike roving glass eyeballs, shadow stealing
everyone around them on cellulose strips of emulsion, better watch out
when floodlights glance off electric teeth of senators, mayors, anybody else
wired for sound, in this moment when the cameras spin frenzy around
their shutters opening & closing like mouths of beached fish
gulping for air (so dance, now, you odd figments created by our own
imaginations, dance when the spin doctors of print & celluloid start
        waving their batons,
orchestrating you—& me—like some cold-blooded conductor
director of the slant & angle of this well-rehearsed, scripted & staged photo
opportunity, grin & wave a hand, kiss some motherless child on the cheek,
wear all kinds of silly caps & hats, but always grin & skin some scheme
we all will see and hear later on, & after the rush dies down, you sap
gushing silly rhetoric, cheap, invented images wrapped in plastic
throwaway grins some spin doctor taught you always to wear)
so we'd better watch out, better learn to click off these fuzzy blinking
blizzard-snow screens blocking out the dreams we will never imagine again
rolling through these moments of sound bits & spin doctors—as we do—
waving batons that control our lives through manipulation
of zippered grins in suits spouting linguistic novocaine that disappears
like throwaway images sucked down black holes of fastfood brains

# A RESPONSE TO ALL YOU "ANGRY WHITE MALES"

eye mean please, already, gimme a break, can we agree to disagree
about who stole all them greenbacks from all them s & l's, who
owns all the major corporations in red white & blue america, who
closed all those military bases,
fired all you "angry white males" in the first place, who
was it, some out-of-work black jigaboo, some poor illegal immigrant
who stole what job from who, or was it your good-old-boy neighbor who
looks just like you that broke your balls—no foolin?—& calls himself buddy

tell me, who runs all the big banks & movie studios in this country, who
owns all the powerful daily newspapers, writes most of the major stories,
shoots us with all this song & dance rapid fire over god's airwaves,
who sits in benches in judgement of everybody, who
brings most of the dope that destroys our children
into this country, who planted the hatred in the KKK, the white Aryan nation
in the first place, who sent all those jews to ovens back in world war two,
who wins the title hands down for being the champion serial killer
on the planet, who lynched all those black & american indian people
just because they could, who's polluting, destroying the ecology of the planet
just for money & property, who wiped out all those american plains indians,
gave them all those doctored-up blankets laced with disease
who bloomed a mushroom cloud over nagasaki & hiroshima, who
unleashed AIDS in central africa, gave us tarzan as king of the jungle,
like elvis got to be "king of rock 'n' roll" after he chained all those black
blues singers to his voice, who complains all the time about this or that
about not getting a fair shake if things don't go their way,
like a petulant two-year-old with their mouth stuck out in a pout,
wearing some cheapo rug toupee on their shiny, bald pates, who do

you do, white boys, that's who, eye mean, is it anybody's fault you can't sky
walk like MJ through space, what do you want, for christ's sake, everything
you done created, all the test-tube heroes as white boys in the first place—
batman, superman, spiderman, john wayne, indiana jones—
inside your own media laboratories

eye mean, whose fault is it you don't believe you've got any flesh-
&-blood "real" live heroes anymore—do tell, shut my mouth wide open—
walking on the planet, eye mean, is that my fault, too

what's the problem here, when you can go right out & make a hero up,
invent all the ones you like with a flick of a TV teleprompter, movie camera
        switch &, voilà,
there you are, all of a sudden you've got a short sylvester
stallone invented bigger to idolize & immortalize forever
as "rocky" through "tricknology"—which elijah muhammad told us once
was your game—who beats up on any man twice his size that comes along,
but especially large black men, when everybody & their mama knows
white men haven't had a real great boxing champion for years,
& you talking about being disadvantaged in everything
because of affirmative action, which you've had all along in the first place,
talking about some myth of a level playing field that's been tilted now
to favor me when everyone & their mama knows
it's been tilted all along to favor you, anyhow,
go tell that simple-simon bullshit to someone else

"eenie meanie minie moe, catch a nigga by his toe, if he hollers let him go,
                                eenie meanie minie moe"

eye mean, please, gimme a break already
eye can't take too much more of this bullshit

eye mean

who bankrupted orange county, passed proposition thirteen—
now all you guys don't speak at once answering these tough, complicated
questions, please, take your time, get it right—who invented computers,
creating all the paper-pushing service empires
that put all you rust-belt blue-collar "angry white male" workers—
& black & brown & yellow & red & female workers, too—out of work
in the first place, though "those people" are not entitled to anger
because they don't count in america these days

{ 207 }

now  let's see, was it "eenie meanie minie moe"
who let the genie out of his bottle so he could grow some more into, say,
a jigaboo-niggra-scalawag, who took the whole nine yards & everything else
that wasn't tied down, maybe it was some indian chief, sioux perhaps,
some ghost returned from the grave disguised as sitting bull,
or a ching-chong-slick charlie-chan chinaman
& his nefarious gang of thieves, maybe a mexican "wetback" perhaps,
or some inscrutable slant-eyed japanese kamikaze businessman
who took away all your sweat, all your live savings, but it wasn't buddy,
no, it couldn't have been buddy, your next-door neighbor,
who looks just like you, & is you,


                              could it,
was it—eye mean, who lied about just about everything imaginable
in this century, & before this century, anyway, back in time to whenever
christopher columbus lied about discovering america—he didn't
because you can't discover anything that was already here
& accounted for in the first place—so please, get serious
for once, give me a break, will ya, just cool it, lighten up
don't be so uptight, go out & get yourselves a good lay, grow up

the world isn't going to continue to be your own private
oyster bed for only you to feed on anymore, you two-year-old
spoiled brat
                    get a move on, "straighten up & fly right"
stop all your goddamn complaining & whining
just shut the fuck up, will ya

just shut the fuck up

EYE CHANGE DREAMS

*for Joe Overstreet, Corrine Jennings & George Lewis*


eye change dreams at 42nd street, times square
as swirling people wearing technicolor attitudes speed
through packed days, carrying speech that machine-guns out
in rhythms equaling movement of averted stares
squares even sashay by quick in flip
mimicking motions, as slick street hustlers roll their eyes around
like marbles searching for hits, lick their chops after clicking onto
some slow-witted hicks dripping spit down their lips
eating hot dogs paid with fifty-dollar bills
in broad daylight—

                                       yeah, tell me about it, trick—

escalator sidewalks moving everything along
so swiftly everyone thinks it's their own feet carrying
      their bodies, grooving to a different song
                        than say, in gloster, mississippi

where time is a turtle moving after a flood has crawled back
into the space it came out of in the first place
hear no beepers here
in gloster, no portable telephones panicking anywhere
only the constant slow humming glide of bloating mosquitoes
as they slide through air & bank in for fresh blood-kills
                  wind-tongue guiding them into the target
                       wobbling on their zigzag ride above bearded

irises waving sword-shaped leaves in the breeze
as if preparing to do righteous battle with anyone or something
like people living in the big apple (their game faces constantly in place—
& they even wear them into bathrooms, so scared to death they are
of running into some cold-blooded rat there
staking out their own notion of territorial space)

{ *209* }

try keeping their fluctuating dreams up to speed
switching up each & every moment, in midtown manhattan,
          manic chameleons
everywhere, here, changing faces at high noon, say,
on 42nd street & 8th avenue, claustrophobic
heat-drenching crowds packed in, in august, locks in on flesh cold
as a triple life sentence served out at comstock—
people here switching up gears, trying to sidestep panic
                          in the middle of slapstick dreams
                                    & in the center of it all

a con man who looks like a swifty lazar, the late hollywood agent,
tools around inside a white rolls royce, peddling gimmicks for old
      false-tooth legends,
who look so bizarre in public devoid of heavy makeup—
comic, even—outside of their dream machines, illusions—
tattered memorabilia the con man peddles at some tacky bazaar
inside a rundown building, in a cobwebbed room, where he hawks
      fading photographs of
zsa zsa gabor in her prime, before she started breaking down
in front of our eyes, wearing all that weird graphic white
pancake makeup over her everchanging face-lifts, masking the dreams
we wear ourselves, inside our switching, ballistic imaginations
bewitching us here as we move through times square
popping with the charge of electrical currents

energy eye imagined this poem having when eye first started writing it
than having to deal with how it slowed down midway through,
when eye hit that part of gloster, a third of the way down,
& tried to avoid all those zigzagging mosquitoes
divebombing in for fresh blood-kills—
my direction moving all over the place after that, changing up the focus,
the rhythm, the way my dipstick lines started composing themselves—
at that point in time, they began making it all up
as they went along, as if they were different musicians improvising
this poem—like the swifty lazar look-alike peddling old hollywood
wonders before the fall, before they became toothless legends,
before they became zsa zsa gabor

this sputnik verbal drumstick—a thing to be eaten
after all—promises way more than it could ever deliver
traveling at the speed of complete bullshit, as it were—

a technicolored times-square attitude, without rhyme,
riding in on a broomstick, heartsick & caustic

homesick for that good old big-apple charge

## SLIPPIN' & SLIDIN' OVER SYLLABLES FOR FUN WITH SOME POLITICS THROWN IN ON THE SIDE

slippin' up on syllables, digital flipflops
on the masterblaster waves, ridin' hiphop hoorays
spacin' through miles's deebop grown up from bebop
underneath echoes of who popped that lyin' brotha
upside his head on a way out trippin' chronic
skyride, movin' against the tide
of soul sista number one—whoever that is
these days, though for me it's always been aretha
by a ton of mouth—so hiphop hooray for days
after scottie pippen sank all them treys
in that 1994 all-star game, frontin' off the media blitz
of shaq o'neal's put-the-funk-on-the-nasty-dunk attack
yo, so get back, brotha, with that ton of gold hanging
around yo linebacker's neck, gold rings stranglin' all yo fingers
gold cappin' all the front teeth in your cartoon character's mouth
eye mean, you look like some kind of new-age monster grinnin'
bodacious as some of those cold mean doo-rags useta look
back in them way-gone days before time changed them up
into a zillion handkerchief-head clarence thomases—
or as amiri baraka once said, "tom as clarence"—radiating
themselves in the microwave oven of the good old conservative
u s of a, grinnin' & skinnin' like old chalk-lip stanley grouch
sweatin' & scratchin' with the heat turned way up under his ass
playing "hanging judge" on black progressives for right-wing zealots
helpin' to blow out the lights in a lot of young brothas' brains—
whose murders, too, are as fractricidal as crack in pipes—
while blow-dried hair clones reading running teleprompters—
copy for network commercials—crack down
heard over TV airwaves on misogynistic gansta rap,
which is OK, if they'd just do the same thing to good old corny arnie
schwarzenegger, bruce willis or sylvester stallone—all wrapped up
in the flag as they tell us they are—
& don't even mention steven segal for uzi-ing all them white policemen—

for real deep-sixed up there on them big silver screens & rakin' in tons
of fresh lettuce greenbacks to stash away in numbered swiss bank accounts—
so, say, yo, what've all you boot-lickin' house knee-grows gotta show
for all that ass-scratchin' liver-lipped talk you shamin' on everyone—
your gas-swollen bellies hanging down over your hangman belts
like blown-up balloons—you torpedo-mouth brigades—
neo-negro conservative correct nests—you are, at best,
panting jack-in-the-box pop-ups, clowns appearing in murder
mouthing black pathology talk-show soap operas—
y'all's claim to fame is blood sucking & money's your game to die for—
so crank it up high as a crack attack on a coon coppin' a plea
bustin' a nut plea on TV, cut it loose, juice, pump up for new word
neologists of death mac attacks, new-jack hip slidin' from the mouths
of homeboys sportin' short nappy dreads, cropped on top & shaved around
edges—lone pigtail drooping down backs—& they look like drooping snakes
atop side-trimmed california mexican fan palm trees & bounce up like giggles
when they walk, like mac daddies scammin' on fly hoochies
clockin' dead presidents, while some are laid back, kickin' it up
gaffled by a one-time okie from knee-jerk muskogee—
"cut me loose," someone screams—a blue-suited badge
messin' with a low-ridin' jean-wearin' hip cross-cultural homey
with his quack-quack cap turned backward, unlaced
black nike-reebop hightops, shufflin' as he dips & jiggles def
chillin', some lean gliding moonwalk, clean for the shakedown
walkin' tough with his syndicate while five-ohs cruise by
in the hood, slamdunkin' high-fivin' jack, mind-fuckin' words
is what this mac is all about, jimmying groves of cadences
is what this poem is gettin' to, slippin' & slidin' over syllables
for fun, break-dancin' with verbs & nouns this poem's on the run
from juba to mozart, from bebop to hiphop, this poem's
on the run, slippin' & slidin' on syllables & digital flipflops
this poem's on the run, on the run, on the run, these words
slippin' & slidin', runnin' off new jack, from the mouth

## & SYLLABLES GROW WINGS THERE

a blackboard in my mind holds words eye dream—
& blessed are the words that fly like birds into poetry—
& syllables attach wings to breath & fly away there
through music, my language springing round from where
a bright polished sound, burnished as a new copper penny
shines in the air like the quick, jabbing glint of a trumpet
lick flicking images through voices there pulsating like strobe lights
the partying dark understands, as heartbeats pumping rhythms hip-
hopping through footsteps, tick-tocking like clocks with stopgap
measures of caesuras breaking breath, like California earth-
quakes trying to shake enjambed fault lines of minimalls
freeways & houses off their backs, rocks being pushed up there
by edges of colliding plates, rivers sliding down through yawning
cracks, pooling underneath speech, where worlds collide & sound cuts
deep fissures into language underneath the earth, the mystery of it all
seeded within the voodoo magic of that secret place, at the center
of boiling sound & is where poetry springs from now
with its heat of eruption, carrying volcanic lava flows of word
sound cadences, a sluiced-up voice flowing into the poem's
mysterious tongue, like magic, or fingers of fire dancing,
gaseous stick figures curling off the sun's back
& is where music comes up from, too, to improvise
like choirs of birds in springtime, when the wind's breath
turns warm & their voices riff off sweet songs, a cappella

# LOOKING AT BOTH SIDES OF A QUESTION
*for Roberta Hill Whiteman & Miles Dewey Davis*


fear ignites as quickly as a butane lighter flame blades up
its gaseous yellow tongue, probes the blanketed edges
of darkness, as a man's snaking shadow splays
before dissolving into the nightwing, a blade of light bevels
a groove through the middle of your long-playing imaginations
& is a moment filled with musical clues, you suddenly remember
voices climbing from a choir of singers, their roots edging
into the sound prints of words you choose
to stitch throughout the call & response language, you mix it all up
concoct a gumbo stew of syllables straddling oceans & color lines—
as melodies of great american songs are confluences—
merging sounds from everywhere in these mississippi river voices
flowing through airwaves—as legs of a person planted on two sides
of a small creek support the weight of the whole body
standing upright—this & that is what this moment is here in america
now—& it has never ever been either-or but both sides of the river
considered—voice & song, stone & flower, water & air, earth & sky,
you & me, black & brown & yellow & red & white in the human
flow, flesh & blood coursing through veins is everything we got
here, this & that & all things beautiful, & ugly too, grown up
beneath this sundown light fused with night & day,
are the only things we know, is all we will remember, see, or hear
now, or forever, at the very edge of this black hole, looming—
a flower suddenly blooming there as quickly as that flaring light
switchblading up snags our attention—like the tongue of a lizard,
a butterfly—perhaps makes us look into the eyes of a deer & see
our own lost love there, dropped somewhere in the past
we came from to here, that me may lay down our cocked guns
& know the fear flaring up quickly there as that lighter's flaming tongue
is what we have become, our own shadows splaying there at the edge
of foaming water, like those of amoebas—star faces spangling above
us—before dissolving into nightwings, blades of light beveling

grooves through the middle of our long-playing imaginations
perhaps hears this moment now as a possibility for music,
clues our voices recognize as a confluence of rivers
the poet shapes, perhaps, the lyrics of new american melodies
that our lives might be joined in a choir singing great songs

# ONE FOR CHARLIE MINGUS

into space-time walks bass strings of charlie mingus
jambalaya rhythms deepening our ears, hear
voices springing from tongues of mingus riding sweet bass strings
deep stepping through sound, through light & shadows of blood
cut out into the leaping night walking music swings the wind
as tongues of evening caress the flying darkness, there
inside rhythms, tight embraces of sound-thump bass grooves
lengthening the graceful flights of cadences shading chords of voodoo
who doing who there, juicing mean watts boys sluicing, shimmying down
mean streets of the city of angels, when mingus played a strange, disquieting
beauty, turned it on, believed in whatever he thought he was back then
played it all the way here, where eye am dreaming now, listening
within this moment of musical amazement, walking in
his voice riding in through vibrating strings thumping & humping
like naked lovers inside musky hot steaming rumpled backwater bedrooms
in the afterglow of undercover damplight, in the nighttime of their dreams
mingus skybreaking his bass through steep blue
lifetimes of urban screams, who doing what to who here
inside the city of lights, raining tears, raining blood & blue showers
electrifying nights where mingus walked music through voodoo
flying all the way home, thumping the rhythms, mingus stalks
the music tone after magical tone, walks the mysterious
music all the way home, tone after magisterial tone

REFLECTIONS

*for Thomas Allen Harris & Nelson Mandela*

1.

the face in the lake's mirror swallows
the sun & moon & stars

on land, at the crossroads of spirits
there is no absolute good, or evil, only chance
& choice of directions to blow

elegba, the trickster,
devil of the cross, intersecting
roads, dividing into chicken bones, wishbones—
crossbones?—of peace, in honor of eschu
celebrant
of the pour cool water dance
at the point
where the roads meet
each other, crisscrossing

black lines

at the meeting point, where
a blood red eye is dropped into a socket
where a bit of earth is scooped out
to form an indentation
for the eye of blood to pool
& turn into a tiny lake, a boule
resembling a stare
of a one-eyed celebrant

a pool of insurrection

there, a ghoul at the moment
of incubation, a fool crisscrossing

himself with blood

2.

go then, brother, sister, go in a lightning
flash, down the road sliver with moonrays
mother, father, uncle, aunt, cousin, friend
go down the road hand in hand
move away from darkness
speak to meet each other here for the first time
with eyes wide open to chance, see
the light that is a sash, a bright blade of shining
steel slitting through the throat of the spirit-filled
darkness, where a moon ray licks over now
a straight road black with houngans
chanting—to wash the way clean—
its bright tongue laying down
a pathway, shimmering

in the night

go, then, spirit, go, go to
where a dry wind is only a passover
now, on the outskirts of vocal
execution, where
words & names roll off tongues
like bombs, or strange bats circling
a room filled with anguish—
a tortured elocution hatched here
in some foreign zip code sitting at the bar
drinking down some sluicing speech that was a passover
ejected from history, where letters of the alphabet
clash now in weird flights, somersaulting
through space, like jet planes
crashing into one another
tumbling through place—

go then to the place where spirits move
& roll magic off tongues, twisting around sounds

of ecclesiastical pronunciation
as if the mouth was filled with so many holy drumrolls
here, shaking tailfeathers from voodoo clear & bombs away
there, in words tattooing themselves into rimshots
bombarding the quivering skins
with back beats, bass tones of hiphop
rapping staccato rhythms & hear lightning cracking
jagged from thunderheads towering overhead & zigzagging
in the west, carrying dark elephant cloud trunks
swinging back & forth & swirling in with a train's roar—
on the other hand, it could sound like a plague of birds whistling
overhead, as in an infestation of verbs—
hear the avenger sweeping in from the west
black & fearsome as a cyclone
it's fury screaming 400 years of smashed skulls
pounded to dust & scattered in an offering

over moonscapes of nuclear-wasted landscapes

hear the rage pumping through the blood
to be transformed into a miracle of forgiveness
& great music taking the high road of cadence & utterance there
mandella of the mantra chanting true & long, man della of the strong
pure sweetness, song, man del la of the great noble gesture here
mandela the storyteller sitting under a baobab tree
kwela carrier of the blues in the form of a nyala
gong & bell ringing like a pure light in your hands, man della
of the shining hour, go forth, mandella of the sweet healing
touch, go forth, nelson mandela, nelson man
del la, go forth with your song
go forth with your light, go forth with your healing
touch, go forth surrounded by light
in all this darkness, nel son
man dela, go forth, brother, go forth

nelson mandela, go forth, brother, go forth

ah oom, ah oom, the sound of didgeridoos
ah oom, ah oom, ah oom, didgeridoos
wa do, wa do, wa do, didgeridoo

ah oom, didgeridoo, ah oom, didgeridoo
ah oom, didgeridoo, wa do, wa do
ah oom, didgeridoo

wa do, wa do, wa do, didgeridoo

nelson mandelas all over the world, come forth
come forth & go forth, come forth & go forth

go forth, spirit brothers, go forth

go forth, spirit brothers, go forth

# COLLAGE

inside its own mystery, the poetic line circles back & forth
moving between & around parameters, shifting questions
like chess moves, words strike at the heart of syntax
everywhere, deploy their chord changes as notes in musical phrases
or cluster like drones silhouetted in a honeycomb if the voice box breaks
& its tone is always dry as bone, its volume mannered, meticulous,
never raised above a humming whisper—but is a thin straight line
cutting through the graph of an EKG heart-monitoring machine
doodad—no accents there, no nuance, no effervescence
as in a spew bursting spumescent from a sudsing waterfall—

the petals of spray holding faces in that foaming articulation there—
when dashed over stones, in swelling deep basin bottoms, fingerlike
plumes dancing upward, when the water hits the surface hard & is bridged
across the light to a shimmering point by a miracle of arching rainbows
where the sun rides up through the transparency of misting flesh
& the veiling water's cloudlike breath is atomized in flicks
shadow catchers pick & catch in black & white or luminous
color frames, shot through their optic lenses, like nirvana
& can be a luminous moment of pure magic when snatched
from a thrilling once-in-a-lifetime moment & is crystallized there

inside an image of what air jordan used to create, when he soared high
above the rest, up there in space, as if he were jimi hendrix, or the prince
of darkness, miles dewey davis playing blue on *aura*—all playing mantras
deep inside themselves, without a clue of bullshit or hesitation,
without fear of switching gears, as they soloed to bloom into flowers
of their syncopated magic, shining, high up above imitations—
their imaginations flying somewhere perhaps out over the dome of montana
where the eyes see clouds as shoes, or bruising battleships
cruising wide open currents of wind, light, skies blue as eyeballs there
of some scandinavian mountain-climber bird-tracking through snow
upward, toward some summit, where *we* fix now *our* arrowing gaze
& where a flock of birds is a burst of syllables—as in a sprinkling of black

notes as winged chords—scattering themselves across our view
as if they were a crew of dark dots tacked to the surface of some painting—
a collage of impressions flung there as if they were a herd of nervous eyes
hyperventilating, as in the body language of new-age hiphop cultural stew,
the colors there dazzling, the aroma of their digable planet mac attacks
sizzling staccatic, pungent inside blooming spices of words flung everywhere
as clues of generational breakdown—what else can eye tell you
except the world is square instead of round, that there's no meaning

to the silly question of if one walks in a straight line or staggers up a hill
but an argument over shape, you know, apples or oranges, skinny or fat,
or the reason some blockheaded gringos slosh beer & act out roles of ugly
americans in mexico, deep inside the microwave oven of their fogs—perhaps
ratcheting up an urge of jeffrey dahmer, a bar or two of nuclear burnout
blues—whacked-out on the bullshit tip of walt disney's mouseketeering trip
& stretched out on sun-fried sands of cash-&-carry brains, oozing madly
all over gridlocked freeways of L.A., every day, hey, we're talking about MTV
informational meltdown here, a blizzard of cardboard images hacked up
& dropped in a frenzied celebration of confetti on a ticker-tape parade—

eye mean, the whole whirl changed after that mushroom cloud bloomed
& left all those incinerated shadows inked into the world's collective brain
but whose children then rose up through schematas of grids & computer
chips to strangle the money flow in the throats of mad bombers
of the west & diverted away a gaggle of greenbacks to their squirrels nests
located somewhere in official tokyo—imitations of cowboys & rockers there
too, at best a weird fascination with the culture of those who bombed them—
somewhere in the west, on a clear day in june, when eyes seem to see
forever, reaching out, covering space from perception to recognition, what is
seen, though, might not always be true, but is only possibility, suggesting

what *might* be true, as in a mirage when our eyes tell us what we see
there, square dancing in front of us, are xeroxed copies of middle-american
porkers, who are copies of other copies of other copies & on & on & on
ad infinitum, though what might be truer is that those copies we think
we see are only white styrofoam sculptures of george segal, unctuous
illusions caught up in shifting light outlining magical tricks the art of seeing

plays on our terrified minds—images grafted there through our eyes
wheedling spin doctors of influence lay down on us—as in a photo of air
jordan, seemingly walking up there, through space, his outstretched arm
& hand holding a basketball, his leonine body a picture of lean beauty

strength & grace & the black & white colors showing no tension at all

AVALANCHE

*for K. Curtis Lyle & the memory of Richard Wright*


within an avalanche of glory hallelujah skybreaks
spraying syllables on the run, spreading
sheets, waving holy sounds, solos sluicing african bound
transformed here in america from voodoo into hoodoo
inside tonguing blues, snaking horns, where juju grounds down sacred
up in chords, up in the gritty foofoo
magical, where fleet rounds of cadences whirlpool
as in rivers, where memory spins down foaming into dances
like storms swallowed here in a burst of suns
up in the yeasting blue voodoo, holding
the secret clues mum, inside the mystery, unfolding
up in the caking dishrag of daybreak, miracles
shaking out earthquakes of light
like mojo hands luminous with spangling
& are the vamping blood songs of call & response
are the vamping blood songs of call & response

as in the pulpit, when a preacher becomes his words
his rhythms those of a sacred bluesman, dead outside his door
his gospel intersecting with antiphonal guitars, a congregation of amens
as in the slurred riffs blues strings run back echoing themselves
answering the call, the voice cracked open like an egg, the yolk running out
the lungs imitating collapsed drums & he
is the rainbowing confluence of sacred tongues, the griot
the devotion of rivers all up in his hands, all up in his fingers
his call both invocation and quaking sermon
running true & holy as drumming cadences
brewed in black church choirs, glory hallelujah vowels
spreading from their mouths like wolfman's mojo
all up in mahalia jackson's lungs
howling vowels rolled off hoodoo consonants, brewing
magic all up in the preacher's run of muddy water
strung all up in the form drenched with coltrane

riffin' all up in miles of lightning hopkins mojo songs
blues yeasting lungs of bird
when music is raised up as prayer & lives
healing as june's sun quilted into black babies'
tongues, sewn deep in their lungs as power
& blueprinted here in breath of rappers

& this is a poem in praise of continuity
is a poem about blood coursing through tongues
is a praise song for drowned voices lost in middle passage
is a praise song for the slashed drums of obatala
is a construct of orikis linking antiphonal bridges
is a praise song tonguing deep in the mojo secrets of damballah
in praise of the great god's blessings of oshun
in praise of healing songs sewn into tongues
inflating sweet lungs into a cacophony of singing
praise songs tonguing deep mojo secrets

& this poem is about music, when music is what it believes
it is, holy, when voices harmonize, somersaulting colors
in flight, & glory is the miracle poetry sings to in that great getting-up
morning, within the vortex of wonder, confluencing rivers, light,
glory in the rainbows arching like eyebrows across suns
glory in the moonlight staring from a one-eyed cat's head
& eye want to be glory & flow in that light,
want to be coltrane's solos living in me
want to become wonder of birds in flight of my lines
want the glory of song healing in me as sunlight
want it tongued through leaves
metaphoring trees, transformed where they seed & stand up here
as people, in this soil, everything rooted here in blood of mother's flesh
& is the poetry of god in deep forest time, singing & listening
& the music there is green, as it also is purple
as it also is orange brown & mind-blowing electric banana
as it is red cinnamon & also again green
sound ground up against lavender
beneath sunsets fusing crisp blue light

& night here stitched with fireflies flicking
gold up against bold midnight & once again, yes,
green, as shimmering caribbean palm fronds
are green in the center of apocalyptic chaos

& my poem here is reaching for that greenness
is reaching for holy luminosity shimmering in gold-
flecked light, where the mojo hand is seaming through
high blue mornings, waving like a sequined glove up in the glory
of hallelujahs, calling through the inner tube lips of the great god
singing, up in the blues root doctors, jacklegging sermons
up in the condolences mourning death
up in the sunburst of god's glory
& eye want this poem to kneel down itself before healing
want it to be magic there beneath the crucifixion of light
want it to be praise song, juju rooted
want it to be mojo hand raised up to powers of flight
want it to be tongue of gritty foofoo, feeding
want it to be a congregation slurring amen riffs
running back through me to you
the voice raised up here, guitar blues licks, holy
want it to be ground earth of resurrection, in you, in me
the bridge tongue of healing is the drum of this song
& it is reaching out to you to cross over
to the sun, is reaching out to touch your heartbeat
there, to become one in the glory
to feel the healing touch
to become one with the glory
this poem waits for you to cross over
to cross over the heartbeat touch of your healing
hands, touching hands, touching hearts
this poem waits for you to cross over
to cross over love, this poem waits for you
to cross over, to cross over love
this poem waits for you to crossover
too crossover, too, love

# LET'S SAY YOU ARE WHO

let's say you are who you believe you are—yellow light
burning delirium in your cat-quick eyes—
& you have imagined yourself more than one time
spread-eagled, caught in the cross hairs of a man's
rifle sight, in the line of fire
so to speak
& that man is aiming
        to erase the blackboard
               of your memory with one true shot
           right between the eyes

& let's say, on the other hand, you're some sad-sack dancing
ghost blabberthoning around some bleached old language
filled with creepy metaphors of werewolves
you sing starring in some opera
& where you see & recognize your true self for the first time in the stunned
faces gathered at the opening night's party
after you skunked up the air
with the blooming storm-clouds of poots
            you oozed & leaked out of your fat

derriere, boxcar, you know,
what some might call your caboose

        anyway

& let's say you are some fly homeboy who likes to count
dead presidents, stacked up high on some cocaine-dusted table
while all around you sound tracks pulsate
to the time of dancing bones anchored to puppeteer's strings you pull
& the overriding melody stitching through the music is one of cracking
gunfire, spitting bullets that remind you of the pungent, full smell
of gladiolas & carnations blooming in the air you inhaled
just last week, at another funeral—how many this year, homey?—

the face there cushioned on a bed of white satin
looked waxed & unreal, the lifeforce gone somewhere
you won't know about until you get there

& let's say perhaps you are someone else who is always lifting up
fluted champagne glasses—full & bubbly—to the memory of himself
standing in the middle of a sentence in history
let's say perhaps it is a saga of the bloody march of the cherokees,
which one of our ancestors penned back when those syllables were strange
sounding—when heard by our ears now, full of british accents, as they were
back then—& desperate to please as, say, those feathers
swirling around that beautiful round ass of josephine baker's way back then
in the closer to now 1920s, over in paris
(& she couldn't do what she did over there over here
for the god-forsaken reasons of some two-faced religious zealots
pushing christian words around while killing & fucking over every one else
on the planet who didn't look like them—& even some of those who did
        look like them—
god, some people are so pious & sanctimonious—
& they seems more so today than they were back then—
well, as they say, some things never seem to change)
what do the words mean you salute yourself with, lifting that glass
so high up into that poisoned air, what does the gesture mean, my friend,
after mushroom clouds have evaporated, like the words your ancestor
pinned on the cherokee nation, reminding me of those yellow badges
nazi germany pinned on jews on their way to auschwitz—
what does it all mean when the light is fading fast from that place
where you stand alone, despite all those grinning fools genuflecting
around you, saluting yourself behind walls topped with broken glass,
a sumptuously set table heaped with food, piled high as stacks
of that homeboy's money on that cocaine-dusted table,
laid out next to where you stand in the wet, poisoned air
as the sad-sack opera star with werewolf metaphors in his voice
spreads around his oozing farts thick as marmalade,
stuffing himself like the pig that he is as he goes,
a sniper lays the grid of his cross hairs on your face
for no reason at all except his random anger

& in the silence of the moment, just before the explosion
let's say you are who you believe you are—yellow
light burning delirium in your cat-quick eyes—
& let's say that, for all intents & purposes
                    & for the sake of argument,
                        we're all in this thing here together,
                            watching each other swarming around
                                swerving & colliding like bats in a cave—

can we stop that assassin's bullet aimed at your head,
my friend, the sniper crouched high up in a tree somewhere
in sarajevo, the red-pouting-lipped
woman poured like a perfect ten into her tight new jeans styled by
gucci, can we stop her from strutting her sweet rolling doobop-
        switching slick-fucking
inner city hiphop quick with her snapping pussy licking clean
some quivering dick, can we stop her from passing that deep seduction on
for a little taste of money
                            my friend,
homeboys stacking paper on their tables
everywhere, people dreaming as they fall screaming
through the burning holes bored in their imaginations
by some random bullet, like the one that is just
about to greet you, my friend

like the one just about to greet you, now

# THE ABSOLUTENESS OF SECONDS

there is time still to consider the absoluteness of seconds
time still even to hear time bombs ticking within words
the metaphors of power swollen
fat behind chewed-up ends of smoldering cigars
the bogus ten of surgically repaired apple-pie white women playing
jane in ever more stupid tarzan movies, red omens circling overhead
like bloodshot moons cocked behind scopes of rifles
zeroing in on stars & bright eyes of babies
time still to recognize those who swear their computerized egos dance
for art instead of money & who sing of cloning as a sacred religion
in place of passion in the wet sucking bloom
& whose art springs from legacies of crosses & ashes
& whose prophecies produce wars & chains & even more bullets

time, still, even to reconsider the trip upriver
from new orleans to st. paul, mississippi-ing the lynched history
passing natchez, st. louis to la crosse, rolling vowels sewn deep
within voices, invisible ghosts whispering along bottoms of the big muddy
the sky above full of blue rhythms & catfish hanging from hooks
barracudas sleeking through the slippery wash underneath the river
time still to listen to those africans
who came here singing
learned here to gut-bucket, fuse bloody syllables into mysterious
hambones, learned here to shape a sho-nuff american blues
into a song full of genius, into a song that embraces love

# BORDERS: IMPROVISATIONS ON A THEME

1.

between the sweetness of beginnings—as in a rush of passion
when two lovers exchange tongues in a greeting of new language
inside the furnace of their mouths, between lips
            after the heat of their desires have first touched—
& the creaking slowdown of endings—as when breaks are applied to
worn-down race cars at the end of the 500-mile indianapolis speed chase
there are moments when time moves as an oscillator
between parameters, between fields of light & darkness
when the pendulum sometimes is a glittering sharp blade swinging
                        back and forth under some leering streetlight
or a huge wrecking ball smashing the chest of an old building—
        on the other hand,
it could be what ears know when they hear seconds tick tocking
that tempo is a locator of movement, as when words arc themselves across
time & space to describe curved backs of sweet women straddling the flow
of a lover's deep stroking when love comes down
            in the secret soft places of an all-embracing night


                                    where the music of the moment creates
rhythms washing wave after wave over fused flesh—
wet & slippery as eels
            swimming downstream in the ebb & flow of currents—


like the soloing of a bright bird flying called miles away dewey davis the third


expression comes together to soar inside interlocking cultures
as fusion explodes xenophobia into crossfertilizations
as when words slip slyly into composition of poetry as jazz notes
become elements of surprise here—in their dancing—
as when feet tap music across dance floors in a response to syncopation
answering the call of antiphonal cadences
            as in the way soukas singers slide their voices
into rapture, enter the shifting music by way of backdoor vibrations

as if inside a seancelike trance, inside a high state of improvisation
the body-voice lifting itself up to curl

                              into worship as heartbeat
as the song of ancestors echoing inside the drumroll of the call
voices of ancestors echoing inside drumrolls of the call
inside homorrhaging of 911 wails of isolation


   2.

we enter the language of poetry in the same way we enter music:
through rhythms of imagination, we are pulled toward doors
to walk through in cadence, in time with something we know or hear
clearly & recognize as something familiar, or unfamiliar but compelling
anyway, the need to go forward & give ourselves over to
the mystery of communication there, choices
                        sounds tumbling over each other pull our ears into the art
of listening & knowing what
we hear is meaning, anchored to some geographic or linguistic soil
              we move toward sound sculpture, slide down slopes of syllables
words flying away like notes or chords in a final cadenza
dancing into rapture
                                & it is here that we lift up colors & objects
        we shape with our tongues inside the caves of our spirits
(like the opening & closing of mouths of beached or robust fish swimming
like graceful birds through liquid flow of underwater currents
is a hint of how long the mystery of breath will last)
inside this oobop-shebop moment of wah-wah rhythm 'n'
blues & jazz, syllables broken off & chewed up in accents
in a mélange of jambalaya tongues circling out to hoodoo
the language, recreating itself daily as it sashays down
american highways imitating the hum of didgeridoos
the circular breathing of john coltrane
the bombing electric guitar runs of jimi hendrix


   3.

the possibility of beauty as an extension of the spirit of language
the ebb & flow of music connected to antiphony as a doorway to magic
woven throughout textures of what we bring to the table of communication

as voices interlocked within cultures of syncopated hip to pelvic movement
recognize rapture far deeper than divinity of stone feet anchored to floors
& see in the glory of a river of butterflies that can summon up mystery
a holiness more profound than the simple acquisition of money
& see an invocation of healing being conjured up there, a dusk song of spring
winds softer than the balm of a lover's sweet tongue—thick & marmaladed
it swells its deepening language of juju probing ecstasy where
we enter the rapture as magicians, ears picking up faint calls of balafons
floating mysterious as a cloud of white broken-winged feathers over
a long highway full of carwrecks that is a metaphor for history


4.

the concept of narrowness can be a set-in-stone old maid, a constant
reminder—view—that the jumping-off point for an olympic platform dive
is a skinny little board propelling a diver up into space
before falling into a sanitized pool of water, the verdict of judges passing
or condemning the diver's effort—at best, a subjective vote, a feeling
one has for the purity & grace of line & shape plunging before them—
this or that—is based on what one remembers
being taught was beautiful, refined even, as form approaches
in some precise singular way, the act of regurgitating cloned memory
what one has become used to as defined by some culturally biased etiquette
a reminder of the old ways, perhaps, the shape & form of why
things were done in a certain way—this pile of shit versus that pile
of doodoo—a sonnet up against free verse, black as opposed to white,
europeans against all unwashed masses, otherness versus civility,
jazz up against classical music—stylized european folk music, really—
ballet or african free-form dance, blues up against country & western
bluegrass as opposed to rhythm 'n' blues, white rock versus funk
& rap, postmodern against beatnik, improvisation
against notated forms, white militias against everybody else
raising the flag for patriotism, against anything & everything
located outside the hip pocket of do you read me now righteousness
the english language versus the american mongrel way
of speaking, the european brass shout against the low juju
of a didgeridoo snaking its voice along damp dirt floors

5.

         & sound can be an arbitrary line drawn somewhere
as a border in the sand of a closed mind, separates
                perhaps
           what is human from that considered different
other, perhaps, evokes a razor slash that rips across the map of a throat
indicates a border dividing life from death in sarajevo
rwanda, is a moment, perhaps, when the heart becomes a torture chamber
of fear, a cave full of dark memories echoing the sight of severed ears
& the legislation of the imagination there complete
in the name of progress,
                where croaking fat toads seated in government gather
     in their reeking latrines called parliamentary chambers
pontificate the way the world is
                greasy as oil slicks
their words spinning around lubricated blades of hovering helicopters
    like clouds of feathers of seagulls or crows, their benefactors
strutting below like so many blustering buzzards

rinsed in white—beneath a full moon surrounding a cross burning
at midnight—all dressed & wobbling to a fools' ball
like wet drunken penguins tracking webprints across sands
of the world that are washed away by incoming tides like their words
swallowed up in the howling wind-blown throat of an avenging god
who never took their deceitful squawking seriously anyway
nor their two-timing priests, all dressed in robes of gold & white
jeweled amulets hanging from their fat wrinkled necks, glitter
like malice, bright edges in the night, after light glances off them
ignites a spark that blazes like cold intent
flashing like a razor in the eyes of some jack the ripper
lurking in the dark gloom of premeditation

so where is the distilled history of memory in all of this, where
the wisdom learned from the reasons that took our children away
left them still as stones in faraway places, inside themselves
dazed looks of surprise & incomprehension
masking their once soft faces, hard now as rigor mortis—like our dreams

for them & for ourselves—their mouths sculpted into shapes of Os we see
spread out in a plague of corpses in some isolated or familiar places
zoomed into dinner hours through constantly blinking idiot tubes complete
with cliche-ridden scripted voice-overs read by plastic grinning puppets
made millionaires & media darlings by puppeteers pulling strings
behind the scenes: are we all lost in some nightmarish
dream, is this the future all our greed bargained for?

skinheads & gin heads rich in hatred for anything that moves
timothy mcveigh in oklahoma city, susan smith in south carolina
jeffrey dahmer in wisconsin & lyle menendez reloading his shotgun
in the city of light & angels & blowing his mother's face completely off
as she lay twitching on the floor from his first shell
& what about the near transaction of nicole's long, beautiful neck
her head left dangling like a full-bloomed rose

                                    from a just-cut stem

all them senseless drive-by slaughters in anywhere america everyday
inner city blues, black & brown & yellow red baby blues rapping
saturday night specials spitting venom poisonous as any mamba snake
"natural born killers" on telly tubes for all the little kiddies to see, rock stars
biting off heads of bats, blood drooling down their lips—serum albumin—
like some modern-day for-real bela lugosi ghoul decked out in some scream-
ing, graffitied T-shirt, trying to run death metal down
& the DNA markings of language up in all of this
are words rooted in some particular space of blood utterance
a sound as cultural as washboard scrapings of blues phrased guttural
as a catholic priest delivering the monotone drone of a liturgical mass
sermon in boston, a silky strand of long straight hair opposed to tight
nappy wrap of lamb's wool curlicues, a gesture, pigmentation of eyes, skin
tones, what composers hear when they dream music under the umbrella
of night, campfires dotting mountains like stars, what they hear
watching sizzling streetlights blinking through the jungle of urban buildings
        like a plague, fireflies
swarming around a volcanic summer's night
is where borders arise from, stretch themselves across
landscapes, like invisible walls enclosing somewhere deep

inside an imagination held tight in a locked-up prison cell—
this & that as opposed to this or that—sometimes blocks off
the possibility of renewal from a moment of revelation
as when time switches up & music hears bebop scatting in after swing
as when rap rhythms informed attitudes of modern yin & yang samplings
of every whim that waltzed in before its heat melted the tip of the ice-
berg of rhetoric, its cadences informing everything, like a runaway
rhyme scheme surfing down the information highways with hiphop
inner-city beats, the meaning of words inverted in attitudes
like caps on bobbing heads turned backward
the different ways that words & rhythms flow now
through intersections, cross-fertilizing old forms
the way old structures are torn down & new ones rise up
in their places quick as instant movie stars vanish after one big flop
the way visual artists see shape unfolding before windows of blinking
television sets kicked in by some rampaging mules loose
in small rooms filled with priceless china
is where we are now, everything turned around, these days
backward as the caps on heads of pissed-off hiphoppers

6.
& what of cross-fertilization of the blood, of gene pools
crosshatching inside wombs of culture, we are what
we are, connected to the veining circuitry carrying through
fire fusing whatever is contemporary with whatever is ancestral
as the merged imagination reconsiders
the beginnings of idolatry shared by global transmissions
short-circuited grief looping back to feed on runaway egos blown
dead in their tracks by reversed goosesteps of revenge
(it's a game of controlling systems we're always in—
though pooling blood genes frequently wins out over creative intelligence—
haikus against sonnets, sestinas up against rondeaus
villanelles against the blues) though in the end
great poetry wins out every time, everywhere it is
the true song living in the bird's commanding flight brings us back
to wonder, exultation, to miles's sweet secrets brought to life here
through ears when trumpeting wind moves leaves & flowers to dance

& sing on branches, not like some wired robot purring electric
but blood of cross-fertilized music at the root is what will carry
the day, a common language full of words flying like birds
to some secret place we know is there, deep inside, meaning
bonded within the shared recognition of a simple gesture


7.

the funkiness of halitosis & gooey toe jam
after days spent sweating up a storm in old reeboks
is something to consider here when we speak
about what the mind imagines when it considers the sense
of smell, what the eyes see & imprint upon the imagination when
the camera of the retina develops the line & shape of surfers
shooting their bodies through curling waves of the banzai pipeline

in hawaii, where sculpted boards carry surfers skiing over fierce
foaming water—that reminds one of a rabid dog's tongue
to catch a giant wave rather than being white-knuckled down
to some 9-to-5 slave, with some bully boss, with both a bad case
of DTs & words that are constantly slitting throats

so bright young california boys take to the waves in droves
glide & ride & strut their stuff across the pacific's liquid stage
standing tall or crouching low, they feel the water through feet
riding balsa wood  & polyurethane boards to the rhythm of rock 'n' roll
guitar licks splashing sounds of dick dale, ride those waves all the way
into glory, stacking up green paper as the rock 'n' roll all the way in
to where some crash the wet black rocks of windandsea, la jolla
& die with the last thought of catching another big ride in their minds
& it is a way of seeing themselves as one riding the spirit of the wave
bringing them here with a beer in hand, a lifestyle full of sun & sand
a kind of language in & of itself, like them, a ritualized metaphor
the tribe understands across borders, waves & sand, the sun as one
music driving the board, the body gliding the way through towering
water, moving low through row after row of miniature tidal waves
crashing & foaming toward shore, always in a state of becoming
constantly becoming, always changing shape & always
becoming, becoming, be coming . . .

the language of poetry in a jet screaming sonic boom overhead
announces that we are always prepared for war & plunder here
complete with professional spin doctors
who stay ahead of the game by telling us all the things we want to hear
no matter the bright light & waves being ridden in by suntanned poets
flashing their lines across liquid stages here
as if they were some strange breed of wingless bird taxiing down
a runway, shooting down the middle of a wave, coiling their bodies up
tight, preparing their spirits to be catapulted into flight

8.
somewhere outside prisons of all this commercialized media hype
ears pick up antelope rhythms of language sweetly seducing
as a breeze strummed from strings of a kora
clocks movements of voices through dreams that straddle land & water
reminds us that music is cadenced by spirits grooving hypnotic heartbeats
vibrating through talking drums

but we also hear the far-flung dismemberment of bodies & cultures
inside music, where some hearts cannot recognize love
cannot recognize the beauty of lalabella in his dream of eleven
stone churches carved out of one rock in ethiopia, thousands gathered there
at sunrise, dressed in white, their voices climbing up rungs of air & light
in exaltation, while out in the desert where sandstorms pick up speed
we can see ten-mile-wide swirling dervishes, screaming, lethal as any terror
gathered up in tornadoes, howling through the fear anywhere thunder
bolts unzip black hoods of skies, somewhere out over middle america
at the intersection of sound—mystery & magic—
memory reconnects with itself, at the crossroads of divination
where blues understand their roots inside the healing sounds of balafons
three-quarters of the way up the artery of america's holy river
the muddy mississippi colored by blood & bones & where eye enter
hear the coded secrets of call & response woven inside this poem

9.
o say can you see the future living in computer screens
we've had more elections to make things better for the greedy
politicians who always need new jump-starts in thievery these days

"o sweet banner headlines, please carry my name
   into fleeting moments of deep fame & real money" is what everyone seems
   to be praying for these days, forget about the pain
   screaming like old maids at night in antiseptic bedrooms needing
                              good old fuck attacks from anyone willing

   just keep the corruption moving for just us, the good-old-boy
   generals like the nuke of gin rich, drinking up salacious
   applause & stuff, waddling through a field of white lilies, willy-nilly
   & bursting out of his rumpled two-piece suit, seem to be saying
   while gruff snorting fat pigs burrowing their long snouts into wet ground
   surround him in washington
   where the close air is always humid with promises nobody intends to keep
   because they were made in smoke—

   filled backrooms
   anyway, where the mouths of greedy piglike men hold
   fat cigars protruding from their mouths like big black dicks—
   brown saliva drooling down their chins—hinged in the pursed lips
   like the one that dangled from the mouth of mafia boss
   two-ton tony galento shot dead in a hail of lead
                              in that backyard cafe in brooklyn

   o say can you see the blood flowing bright as red stoplights
   people speed through every day
   as the world gives birth to baby farts who grow up to become replicas
   of elvis presley & madonna, who are always being crowned
   king or queen of something, just rewards—for just them?—
   for stealing everything in the world's house that isn't tied down—
   it all belongs to them anyway for just being born
   is what their spin doctors tell us in so many words wearing earnest
   straight faces, masking buttoned-down attitudes everyone takes
   for pure naivete & innocence, until their guns begin barking sudden death
   tracks stitching rat-a-tat-tat into the rest of us otherized nightmares around
   the whirl & throughout the west, skinheads
   & bible-waving good-old-boys & girls in homegrown militias

spout their anger, their fire & brimstone words—a pint of jack riding
in their back pockets for courage, some demerols secreted in purses
for bouts of whatever—& dementia spreading like out-of-control
wildfires through brains of just about everyone

& it's late & getting later in the game of what we're all gathered here for
as so many immigrants from so many song & dance routines it's hard to believe
so many rhythms & wordplays you can hardly shake a stick at
just one, inside the crucible of culture, a common language is forming
that will shape & define us all as one in the hearing of rhythms moving out
like those spreading out from the center of the river in circles like mantras
we see when a rock has been dropped through flesh
of the water, there, soft ripples moving in waves across our faces
gentle as love songs, beautiful as birds banking down in steep flight
to land in the middle of the light surrounding our profiles
gathered here, where we stand looking into the river singing—
a collage of different skin tones mixing in the water—
our voices climbing in a harmonized confluence of utterance
arching like a rainbow across storm clouds of western skies

10.
in the midst of the saying, the song
in the midst of the song, beauty
climbing up from the voice to resonate
in air, wrap itself around a rhythm carrying
music, carrying cadence, carrying whatever
the magic is, mystery in the saying
inside the voice, the power of utterance
inside time seeking time
seeking the hidden fascination of an american
image of you, in me, inside the feeling of the marvelous
inside the spirit of you & me, inside the blues moment
of creation, movement inside new miracles
hoodooing new songs, we inside the clues wooing
daybreak from the slackening grip of midnight with the cock's
crow, cacadoodledooing, in the crack of first morning

light, inside the cool murmurings
of water seducing the tongue of your face
jumping up sad or bright from the river
to meet your eyes when you look down there
into ripples, moved by rain or wind
lightening & you there in the undulating waves
like those in a black man's marcel-conked hairdo
greased back in the pomaded pompadoured mad forties
you there in the bleed of lewd secrets
of the moment seeking whatever it was that got away
from you, from me, there, come whatever, time is
what it is, whatever the cadence is, come whatever
time seeks the pulse inside the rising voice spreading out
inside the imperfect voice seeking perfection
in the continuous uttering, inside the magic of secrets
voicing mystery through journey of the poem
that never gets written right
this & that as opposed to this or that
both sides of the river cradling longing
both sides of a question posing other questions
instead of one, the beauty of foofoo, sushi & feijoada
french cooking & chinese cuisine
this & that & music fusing sound to song with syllables
slipped from everywhere, come spirit
come magic, come love
slipped from everywhere, come wisdom, come blood
spilled from everywhere, come light, come darkness, come
floods washing in from everywhere, bring music played
by two hands pulling rhythms from drums
two hands gripping oars of boats moving downriver
this & that fusing two sides of an equation in a question
mark, the rising of many many secrets instead of one there
many faces in the flow of the shape of rainbows
revelations everywhere saying who, saying what, saying you & me
cradling the mystery everywhere, inside the slow pull of miracles
inside the rising tide of magic is where poetry comes from

then & now & again in the future, say who say you
say us in the mystery of the flow of syllables
inside the juggernaut of american language—not english—in the journey
of most most poems flowing out here that most times never get written right
now & forever the mystery in the flow of faces that never get toned right
now & forever inside the skin cloning sadness
inside the machine gun of feeling that kills
the spirit & is never ever done right
but the rush of glowing love pulls us, the beating heart
extended in a handshake here, blessed with the kiss of eyes
tender as a newborn baby's sigh, is what the tongue is searching for
inside the sticky wet furnace of the mouth swapping tongues
spit, is where words come from, turn over the sweet
tongue inside the cave of the mouth, burning
is where language springs from like lava erupting
from a volcano, hot & luminous, powerful & new, transforming
as the crossfertilization of beliefs of priests & rabbis & shamans
holymen sitting across from preachers & medicine men
& imans & buddhists in america, the holy ghost
crisscrossing tongues, this & that in a fusion of you & me
& everyone in a flowering of we in this moment
where we live in the here & now & forever inside
the magic of singing in the flow of the mysterious cadence
inside the rowing consonance of the impudent river
clean or dirty water washing smooth ripples across our faces
as we raise ourselves up clean inside our own american voices
holy throughout the sound of its utterance
inside the midst of the saying, the song inside the song
the beauty climbing up from the tongue to the level of utterance
voice there in the shaping wrapping itself around a rhythm
voice there fused with connections, raises itself up to cadence
& light, carrying the music of geography & place
the voice moving out in ever widening circles like a mantra
creating inside its own mystery & magic a unique genetic voice
inside a celebration of opposites & contradictions
you & me in the fusion of the utterance, you & me

inside the tonguing love, you & me inside this volcanic
love transforming, inside this sweet moment of hesitation
before we go on forever in the magic of forgiveness
you & me as we inside this sweet tonguing moment
you & me as we embracing forgiveness in the here & now
inside this sweet moment of forgiveness
you & me fused, inside the here & now

UNTITLED


speed is time clocking itself
birth to death
          seconds beating quick
as heartbeats thumping

drums in cadences
imitating breath


CHUCKANUT DRIVE,
SOUTH OF BELLINGHAM, WASHINGTON


south of bellingham
poplar trees shoot leaves skyward
golden, late autumn
firs, ash & broadleaf maples
umbrella the curving road


SAN JUAN ISLAND IMAGE


ride chuckanut drive
through mist rolling off puget
sound, san juan islands
pushing through fog, humpback whales
rocks sat down on a mirror

BACK TO THE DREAM TIME:
MILES SPEAKS FROM THE DEAD
  *for Miles Davis (1926–1991)*


back to the dream time, through rivers of sound, eye swim back new
through metaphors of blues, rising from gruff throats of shamans, here
eye rise up like smoke, mix with their voices slurred over guitar

riffs like balm, cascading clues of their syllables dropped
from the sun stone of their songs, images dropped like severed heads
from hooked beaks of giant prehistoric birds blowing fierce winds & fire

& as if by magic, eye have come here to this antiphonal call of language
to see shadows wrinkling like winged scarves, undulating sideways
like swift snakes crossing the desert of imagination

have come here to drop the blue notes of my trumpet voice
into this snake pit of silence (which is the sheerest void of darkness
anywhere, where even the sun is a well-kept secret & the moon wears a face

so inscrutable the light doesn't even know its own editing, here, in this place
in this space of transparent echoes) where vowels roll off tongues
like muffled blasts of land mines tattooing the silence

of dream time here & the light over there, on the other side of waking up
besides the trickster figure of myself when eye knew no contradictions
anywhere in my life of a "bitches brew," my spirit hung hip

bop slick from magic of my voodoo, lyrical phrasing, my voice edited
back to almost an absent whisper, to that of these shamans who know
time is a fixed mystery, pulsating wherever it goes

## LA JOLLA

living out here, calm, on the edge of the streaking western whirl
where most sunsets leave vivid stains on the thin black line
separating the pacific from the plunging ocean of flight

above it, time stretching as a peacock's tail feather
through a landscape crisscrossed with colors of bright rainbows
stitched & weaved through green light luminous with complexions

where kite strings split in half a swallowing blue sky leaping
as blue music heard anywhere, voices buried deep in hushed distances
beneath windswept pines whose leaves serenade throughout valleys

& dipping hillsides, as overhead hot air balloons cruise
like great bowheaded whales swimming underneath serrated edges
of bouffant gray-white clouds that look like huge battleships

& where the eye locates on the brow of some precipice a glass
house, that is an atrium—& wondrous beyond all comprehension—
where the sky is a roof, the pacific a glittering blue veranda

swelled with surfers & salt waves terracing in one foaming wave
after another, swimmers bobbing up there like red apples in a tub
at a halloween party, just offshore, while up in verdant hills

golden with light, runners jog up & down streets as nervous people
behind walls & signs reading "armed forces" sit fingering triggers
of shotguns, their eyes boring in tight as two just-fired bullets

## THE FLIP SIDE OF TIME

there is nothing on the flip side of time but more time
yawning, like a cat's wide open mouth of space
above us, around us, dilating like out mother's wombs

just before we came out screaming catching our breath
& found ourselves breathless, bent out of shape with rage
after being cooped up asleep for so long & now all this light

searing here where before all was darkness & now this slap
that wakes us up with such a start, as if it were necessary
since most of us sleepwalk all out lives until death

anyway & sometimes we find ourselves somewhere
hanging from the spur of the moment, barely awake, caught
between twilight & pitch black, perhaps hanging there

from the spur of some island somewhere off the cowboy boots
of italy, looking at a full moon submerged beneath crystal blue
green waters of the mediterranean, ionian seas & the moon

laughing there, like an alka-seltzer tablet winkling at the bottom
of a clear glass of water, our eyes telescoping from above
trying to decipher the mystery smiling from that magical face

but mystery & magic is what pulls our lives toward meaning—
beauty & wisdom discovered inside all heartfelt joy
what journeys reveal, poetry there inside every moment

# FLIGHT

at sunset across a western horizon, bright mauves, oranges & purples
streak with pure speed of broomstrokes, in a glowing ed clark painting
that is a hamburger patty between buns of dark earth & sky

& the pacific ocean stretched out there is a moment deep inside
history, is perhaps a man telling the world what his eyes do not see
where the coastline of california is a necklace of pearls

& diamonds roped like a noose around the throats of harbors beneath
the oozing night, spreading now, from top to bottom
like a squid's amoeba ink, or whatever our vision imagines

there, now, the light sinking fast past canada & alaska to the north
& swallowed whole there in the fish mouth of the pacific, where the sun
is replaced by the vision of a ping-pong ball sticking to the wet black wall

of a room freshly painted & it looks like the moon positioning itself there
outside this airplane window, its mysterious, ghost white face centered
inside our imaginations, where winds seem still but blow fierce

as the jet-stream tongue of a great poet's blowtorch breath
fires cadences of looping saxophone miracles deep into our lives
stretch them into lines where heartbeats are caesuras

arresting speech in the middle of a sentence, like a glorious sunrise
back in the east, at dawn, stops us in our tracks, light there suddenly
breaking the darkness, pure & sweet as a baby's sweet breath

# STILLNESS

underneath a midnight sky, fresh snow rests still & white
as a summer cloud formation, stretching there, soft as a bed
of just-picked cotton, beneath tailfire of a streaking jet

& soon the wind will stir up again the murmuring dead voices
lying there, beneath that blanket of chilled glittering crystals
reminding of light refracting jewels covering the earth's hard floor

the tongue-lashing speech of god's sawblading breath is quiet now
so soon, again, after the cold shattering cacophony of language
an avalanche brings, the sound deafening in its power

& louder than the scream of god inside the voice of a shattering
tornado, louder than roaring screams sudsing in the curling finger
at the top of a swelling epiphany, above the wall of water

howling in a tidal wave, drowning everything within the blink
of an instant, the frenzy suddenly leveling off flat as quick as it came
& now lies there a dark still pool mirroring as in a dead duck's eye

wide open there, as if it were a midnight sky holding a full moon
above a whispering chilled landscape sculptured by hands of winter
the snow swept up into heaps & shapes by god's tongue there

reminds of sleeping polar bears huddled together when seen
from above: scattered around still lifes, the wind picking up snow
swirling it like confetti—voices as if torn away from history

## BIRTH FORM: TERCETINA

underneath a still life snapshot of grass & rocks, probing light
reveals layer after layer of buried history, there, under beds
of earth's terraced graves, skulls & bones out of sight

in darkness, where a symphony of silence echoes the dead
after sonorous beauty of their voices took flight
after the DNA of their flesh melted away, after all speech was said

& done, the drumscript light fingers played on skinheads pulled tight—
as music improvised anywhere—faded away old rhythms inside our heads
as drums insinuated on the other side of this circular moment, right

here, underneath this place, where a choir of trees stands now & leads
is a soft vein of gray & blue beneath & inside the earth's hot night
where history can be an echo of itself after fleeing time bled

throughout the concave dome breath lost to the great sheer height
of night, where now a new form is being born, this tercetina that sheds
light & birthskin in the process of being torn from this slight

moment time gives us, the uncertainty of creation here, form wedded
inside the blood of ancestral language, this terror of shape, this fight
to keep alive a memory, before sweet tenderness bled

itself to death, staining this concrete modern place of blight
& ice, here where music filling skies is thunder & gunshots played
all around our children, their eyes wide open in fear, but bright

# THE VIEW FROM SKATES IN BERKELEY

*for Oliver Jackson, homeboy & painter*

the clouds were mountains that day, behind the real mountains,
sideways, from san francisco, across the tossed bay, the beauty we saw
from skates, in berkeley, was real there, stretched out, behind sailboats
the wind-driven waves buckling, like rodeo horses carrying cowboys
breaking across the foaming gray water, like sand dunes

rippling across an empty expanse of desert, mirrored & beautiful
here, near sunset, we looked out through the wide open windows & took in
the view, unbroken from here, under sinking sunlight, the hills breasts
the gulls resembling small planes, banked over the waves, searching for fish
they snapped up in their beaks, under fleecing clouds

streaming up high, crossing the jet stream, the pricking mist hung low
over angel island, like the day after too many drinks fogged up your head
in an afternoon sunlight, on a day further back in cobwebs that you care
to remember, but there anyway, as a still life you clung to once
deep in a long-gone memory, the skyline changing now

behind the tumbling clouds, the architecture trembling through the mist
of the "shining pearl by the bay," grown up from split-open gums of the land
like chipped shark teeth, or tombstones leaning white & bright
into the light, shimmering, like the friendship of this meeting is shimmering
here, because we knew we were what we always thought we were

homeboys on top of our games laughing like joyous paint in sprayed mist
the fog overhead hung low, over oakland, thick as a mattress
where you laid down your head full of dreams & painted images in full view
of the bay bridge, stretching, like one of your elegant lines through our view
here, outside skates window, the sun plunging like one of your painted

faces into rabid wash of gray waves, the wind slapping salt tears across
our faces, creased, as the american flag is streaked with a rainbow of colors
here, where we were what we always thought we were, on this day

when the moment heaved up the water, surging, like our dreams
& we were riding those bucking horse waves breaking across

the duned, kicking waters, mirrored & beautiful, we were strong
as we always knew we would be, our view unbroken from here, in skates
under the dazzling sunlight of our dreams, streaming across the jet stream
high up in the turbulent afternoon of our heads, light & luminous
we were homeboys, oliver, on this rare shimmering day filled with flight

homeboys, oliver, on this rare shimmering day filled with light

7

---

FROM CHORUSES, 1999

# SONG

words & sounds that build bridges toward a new tongue
within the vortex of cadences, magic weaves there
a mystery, syncopating music rising from breath of the young,

the syllables spraying forward like some cloud or mist hung
around the day, evening, under street lamps, yeasting air, where
words & sounds that build bridges toward a new tongue

gather, lace the language like fireflies stitching the night's lungs,
rhythms of new speech reinventing themselves with a flair,
a mystery, syncopating music, rising from breath of the young,

where the need for invention at the tongue's edge, high-strung,
at the edge of the cliff, becomes a risk-taking poet who shares
words & sounds that build bridges toward a new tongue,

full of wind & sun, breath feeds poetry from art's aqualungs,
under a blue sea that is sky, language threads itself through air
a mystery, syncopating music, rising from breath of the young,

is a solo snatched from the throat of pure utterance, sung,
or wordsmiths blues-ing cadences, weaving lines into prayers,
words & sounds that build bridges toward a new tongue—
a mystery, syncopating music, rising from breath of the young

# SESTINA FOR 39 SILENT ANGELS

there was no screaming to announce hale-bopp comet's second tail,
no screaming when those 39 people left their bodies—
their containers—behind, covered their faces with purple
silk shrouds, folded triangles, lay down smiling & fell into the steep sleep
marshall applewhite had prescribed for them deep inside that death
mansion in rancho santa fe, they knew themselves as angels,

sleuths at creating web sites, cruising the internet, space angels
flying on wings of ancient dreams upward to hale-bopp comet's tail,
(& the only way to get there through the invisible doorway of death)
launched through skies of their minds, they willed their bodies
on earth, as people of jonestown did, to be recycled through sleep,
bodies board-stiff & bloated, looking for peace, skin purple,

going black as the clothes they wore, covered 39 faces with purple
symbols the color of lenten holy week when jesus rose up to join angels,
39 travelers wore black nike shoes, weaved through 39 catacombs of sleep,
dreamed themselves up like 39 shooting stars to hale-bopp comet's tail
of silver ice, where they would transform their bodies—
18 buzz-haired castrated males, 21 females surfing death's

internet—to pass through heaven's-gate's needle eye—& death
not even a stopover here for these souls to rest dressed in black & purple,
quarters for phone calls, 5 dollar bills for whatever urges their bodies
needed—before flying through space 39 dreams, they would be truly angels
rendezvousing with the mothership hidden inside hale-bopp comet's tail,
live with extraterrestrials there in a sleeve of silver ice after sleep

cut them loose to flow through steep mystery above as sleep
like rocket fuel fell away over stages, left them asphyxiated in death
after phenobarbital, apple sauce, & vodka, they knew the silver ice tail
as the sign they were waiting for to cover themselves with shrouds of purple,
leave behind computer screens—skies—they flew purely as angels
now toward a higher source than conflicting urges of their bodies—

a tangle of web sites, conquered & controlled, their bodies—
surrendering the improvisation of living, they swam in sleep,
drifting slowly as motorless boats on the sea—were homeless angels,
took 39 pot pies & cheese cakes for their journey, they kissed death
hard with dry mouths, 39 people down from 1000, pursed lips of purple
open in wonder, they flew up to enter hale-bopp comet's tail

of silver ice particles, gaseous bodies grinning there like death
skulls flashing inside sleep, inside where eye am dreaming now of purple,
faith flashing bright as new angels inside hale-bopp comet's third tail

# FORTY-ONE SECONDS ON A SUNDAY IN JUNE, IN SALT LAKE CITY, UTAH

*for Michael Jordan*


rising up in time, michael jordan hangs like an icon, suspended in space,
cocks his right arm, fires a jump shot for two, the title game on the line,
his eyes two radar screens screwed like nails into the mask of his face

bore in on the basket, gaze focused, a thing of beauty, no shadow, or trace,
no hint of fear, in this, his showplace, his ultimate place to shine,
rising up in time michael jordan hangs like an icon, suspended in space,

after he has moved from baseline to baseline, sideline to sideline, his coal-face
shining, wagging his tongue, he dribbles through chaos, snaking serpentine,
his eyes two radar screens screwed like nails into the mask of his face,

he bolts a flash up the court, takes off, floats in for two more in this race
for glory, it is his time, what he was put on earth for, he can see the headline,
rising up in time, michael jordan hangs like an icon, suspended in space,

inside his imagination, he feels the moment he will embrace, knows his place
is written here, inside this quickening pace of nerves, he will define,
his eyes two radar screens screwed like nails into the mask of his face,

inside this moment he will rule on his own terms, quick as a cat he interfaces
time, victory & glory, as he crosses over his dribble he is king of this shrine,
rising up in time, michael jordan hangs like an icon, suspended in space,
his eyes two radar screens screwed like nails into the mask of his face

# CAN YOU CHAIN YOUR VOICE TO A RIVER?

woke up one morning, found myself stepping through a dream,
say eye woke up one morning, found myself singing in a dream,
eye was on a road long & narrow, the wind was imitating a scream,
the road eye was on was long & narrow, the wind a substitute for a scream,
so eye kept right on walking, hoping the scream would end,
say eye kept right on stepping, hoping that dream would surely end

in the middle of that dream found myself by a long snaking river,
say in the middle of that screaming dream found myself by a long snaking river,
say that river was sky-deep, moonrays dancing off its back like slivers of silver,
that's when eye ask myself a question, a cool wind making me shiver like liver.
say eye ask myself a question, cool wind making me quiver & shiver like liver

said, "can you chain your voice to a river, swim it to wherever it ends?"
said, "can you chain your voice to a river, swim it to wherever it ends?"
rivers carry their own rhythm, carry their own deadly sins,
say rivers are their own rhythm, are their own deadly sins,
blue skies & storm clouds be hats eye wear, wear till the bitter end,
say blue skies & black clouds be hats eye wear, wear till the wailing end

then eye was walking land by the river, caught up in a surrealist dream,
say eye was walking land beside that river, inside a surrealist dream,
when all of a sudden a cloud hung down, spoke to me in the voice of a poet,
say a dark funnel cloud hung down, spoke to me in the language of a poet,
at first eye heard the voice of Moses, then eye heard God up in that wind,
say first eye thought it was Moses, then eye heard God up in that wind

"go downriver," the Voice in the wind said, "go down it to the very end,
eye say take a boat & go downriver, sail it long to the very end,
listen to a broken man singing from a treetop, listen to his ancient sins,
say listen to a poor man moaning on a tree branch, singing about ancient sins,
that old man was once a great singer, ain't heard him since way back when,
that man used to be a great poet, ain't seen him since way back when

now he weak as a puff of smoke, caught up in a tornado's wind,
say he weak as a wisp of smoke, caught in a tornado's wind,
long ago he was handsome & proud, voice stronger than most men eye knew,
say he was handsome, proud long ago, voice better than most men eye knew,
then hard times came on him like he a vampire caught out in daylight-wind,
say bad times caught him like he a vampire locked outside in sunlight, wind
so he ran away, went underground, found himself in that old gnarled tree
say he ran away, went underground, found himself stuck in a gnarled old tree,
now he need to be talked down out those leafless branches, so he can sing again
say he need to be talked down out those skeletal branches, so he can sing again
need someone show him the light, convince him there's a better road,
say he need someone to be his friend, show him there's a much better road,
it's you my friend can show him that light, help him drop his heavy load,
say it's you my friend can show him light, help him drop his heavy load

so go downriver & find him my son, tell him he can swim & sing again
say go downriver, find him my son, tell him we need him to swim & sing, again
but the only reward eye can promise you will be a song you hear up in the wind,
say the only thing eye can give you will be a song you'll hear up in the wind,
a song you keep locked in your heart, make you feel good whenever you hear it,
a song you keep locked in your heart, make you feel good each time you hear it,
so go on downriver, find that man, listen for the song up in the wind,
say go on downriver, find that man, listen for that song up in the wind,
when you find him my son you'll hear yourself singing a sweeter song,
say when you find him my son you'll find yourself singing a more lyrical song"

after getting over shock of hearing that voice eye get in a canoe, go downriver,
say after getting over shock, hearing that voice eye get in a canoe, go downriver,
my life spared by luck & chance eye paddle to a poor man up in a treetop,
bad luck with him to the bitter end,
say my life spared by luck & chance on the river, eye paddle to a man in a treetop,
& him drinking bad luck to the very end,
so eye ask him; "can you make your voice a river, swim it wherever it goes?"
said, "can you turn your voice into a river, ride it to wherever it goes?
rivers carry their own rhythm brother, take you, maybe, to a better close?"
said, "rivers carry their own rhythm brother, might ride you to a better close"
he look at me, then he sang this song, "river, river, take my dreams,

carry them through my poems to sing,
river, river, carry my dreams, teach them how to swim & sing,"
sang, "let me chain my voice to you river, swim your currents to the very end,
eye say let me chain my song to you river, swim your rapids to the very end,
let me see bright day breaking through rain clouds, listen to sweet birds sing,
say let me see bright day breaking through rain clouds, hear sweet birds sing,
& sing to the bitter, bitter end

Lawd, Lawd, thank you Lawd, for letting me sing a sweet, sweet song again
Lawd, Lawd, thank you Lawd, for letting me sing a sweet, sweet song again

let me be a fish, now in your river, swimming downstream all day long,
say let me be a fish in your river Lawd, swimming downstream all day long
thank you Lawd for bringing this boy to help me get down out of this tree,
eye say thank you Lawd for bringing this boy to help me get down out this tree
my blues done taught me how to sing brand new & swim in the river, long,
say these blues done taught me to sing brand new, swim in the river, long, long
Lawd thank you Lawd, for letting me swim in this river, sing a new sweet song,
Lawd, Lawd thank you for letting me swim your river, sing a new, sweet song,
gonna pick up my old guitar today, & sing & just play along,
yes, gonna pick up my old guitar today, & sing & just play along
'cause eye chained my voice to Your river, learned to sing & swim, again
say eye chained my voice Your river, Lawd, learned to swim & sing again,
yesterday was a bitter, cold memory, but today a brighter & sweeter day.
say yesterday was a bitter, cold memory, but today is a bright, sunny day.
eye'm gonna swim my voice down this river, singing to wherever it ends,
say, gonna chain my voice to this river, Lawd, swim it to wherever it ends,
'cause eye'm a fish now in Your river, swimming downstream all day long
say eye'm a fish now in Your river, Lawd, swimming & singing all day long
my voice done took to water now like rain drops falling out of black clouds,
say my voice done took to water, like rain drops falling out storm clouds

so eye thank you my friend for help getting me out of that treetop,
now listen for my song up in the wind
say thank you my friend for talking me down out of that old treetop,
listen for my song whistling high up in the wind,
blue sky the hat eye wear now, cocked ace-deuce to the singing end,
say blue sky the hat eye wear now, cocked ace-deuce to the wailing end

so thank you great Lawd for letting me grow these fins & wings,
say thank you great Lawd for letting me grow these fins & wings,
& thank you friend, for helping me be myself again,
say thank you friend for bringing me Spirit, so eye can sing, again"
then he jumped into the river, began to sing & swim downriver,
say he jumped into the river, began to sing & swim downriver
eye jumped in my canoe, began to paddle upriver, going the opposite way,
say eye jumped in my canoe, began paddling upriver, in the opposite way,
while going upriver eye hear a voice singing beautiful up in the wind,
say as eye was on my way back upriver hear a sweet voice up in the wind

& eye knew it was the song the great Spirit told me eye would hear,
say eye knew it was the song the great Spirit said eye would surely hear,
so eye said;

"thank you great Lawd, for letting me walk around with this song
  locked in my heart,
  say thank you O Lawd for helping me walk around with a poem
  locked in my heart,
  that voice will be in the poems eye write & hear every day
  & eye hear it strong,
  say that song will be the cadence of poems eye write & hear every day
  & eye hear it real strong
  thank you Lawd for giving me the gift to write these poems,
  eye say thank you O Spirit for giving me the gift to write these poems,
  for chaining my voice to a river of syllables, giving me fins & wings
  for chaining my voice to a river of syllables, giving me fins & wings

  thank you great Lawd, for these syllables & poems
  thank you great Spirit, for these syllables & poems

  eye'm gonna swim in the river of this language with my fins & wings,
  & eye'm gonna swim all day long
  say eye'm gonna swim in the currents of language, with my fins & wings,
  say eye'm gonna swim all night long

  thank you great Lawd, thank you
  thank you great Spirit, thank you"

# GRAY DAY IN JANUARY IN LA JOLLA

*for Porter Sylvanus Troupe*


the day absent of sun, troubles in over plush hilltops
threatening rain, cool hours mist toward noon
wearing gray shawls of vapor, patches of blue peek through
ragged holes punched in clouds, look like anxious eyes of scandinavians
worrying through their skins when they see snowstorms coming,
in a place cold & white as anything imaginable, eye look

past green foliage touched with hints of autumn shivering
like a homeless white man in a harlem doorway in february,
look past white ice storms freezing the nation, all the way to the capitol,
on martin luther king day, standing there on heated stone, bill
clinton takes his second oath of office, as rumors swirl around him
posing as vultures devouring an abandoned blood kill,

he lays out a vision for the future as good old boys dumped
like pillsbury dough into their rumpled suits fight back yawns, eyes
boring into the back of clinton's head like cold barrels of shotguns,
the cheers of the massive crowd punctuated by gun salutes,
tries beating back the cold of this day sweeping in from the arctic,
flags popping trembling wings crack over the capitol,

as jessye norman takes us where we have to go, singing:
america, america, God shed his grace on thee, & crown thy good
with brotherhood, from sea to shining sea
but we remember the reality of ennis cosby's senseless death, on this day
out here in the west, where everything seems so cozy & warm, where
time wears the laid-back attitude of a surfer crouched on a board,

riding an incoming wave, eye see climbing up invisible ladder rungs,
deep in his imagination, the growing power of my son
porter's angular body, all arms & legs now, eyes peering out innocent
but knowing, laid-back but cold, his mind calculating the distance
his thirteen-year-old body must conquer before he understands
the meaning of roads he has just walked over pigeon-toed,

{ *265* }

clouds breaking across tops of hillsides, light shimmying in golden
blue, the sky widening into this moment bright as anywhere
clear & warm, the voice of jessye norman touching the blues breaks through
radio, her voice evoking history washes through this poem,
implants hints of lady day's warning of "strange fruit,"
as the threat of another storm gathers itself—as love

& hatred everywhere—north of here, above san francisco,
porter & eye see shadows of clouds lengthening here in la jolla,
see them spreading down hillsides like dark amoebas, mirth,
ragged as edges of daylight slipping toward darkness,
the air cool with mist now, the hour decked out in gray shawls,
cloud vapors now puffing up into shapes of dolphins, whales,

sharks cruising a sky cold as these waters off the coastline

# TIME LINE OF BREATH & MUSIC
*for Richard Muhal Abrams*


fragments blocked out in the air of a sentence,
a man on the other side of a time line
is breathing music up inside silence, is listening too,
the speech of chords riffing from top to bottom,
inside the melancholia of a moment,
back in the zone when space was caught up in the beauty
surrounding singing, the great voice anchored deep within
song, its branches running way down into the soil itself,
where the roots of trees snake their fingers down
like music branching out from different sources
to become song, to become elements of magic
climbing winged compositions of breezes,
carrying flagged newspaper pages flapping
their stingray images above, overhead, cracking
& whipping sound before they split in two, as couples do screaming—
twin birds flying in opposite directions—when they break apart
like atoms, before each fragment splits apart quick
as a note or chord sliced off the solo of a pianist's blurring fingers,
when the music block steps its way into mathematics,
pulls apart, comes back together again, is elastic

moments when breath & music kiss elusive
as mystery, the sound always shifting
the bull's-eye target, an illusion created for ears
weaves a tapestry of footsteps clopping over cobble-
stone streets, somewhere back in all that history, as here, where
a man sits high up in the gabled leaves of his imagination creating
inside a womb of silence, where a syntax of wings & breath is
translated into the language of stop & go traffic
lights, flashing divas, cornucopias shaped
like goat horns blowing out an endless supply
of edible solos, moments are sliced off like shaved glass

slivers of light, glancing off & cutting through the dark
moments of shade, like voices free-falling in time,
they lay their grids of expression over
the night or day in a time line of breath & music,
become melodies of this life that we hear & sing

## TWO FOR THE PIANO PLAYERS
## AT THE SPRUCE STREET FORUM

*for Mike Wofford and Anthony Davis*

I. MIKE WOFFORD'S SET

long-distance words peel themselves through dreams,
peal themselves like bells or wind chimes,
cascading crystal piano runs waterfalling over bosendorfer keys,
just as the fecund imagination of a solo pianist weaves a tapestry,
images sew themselves inside his tap-dancing fingers riffing out sound,
chords caressed from black & white ivory keys spool out,

along an imaginary
clothesline of sound, threads musical lines into space
& it reminds me of a piece of silk thread fed through the eye of a needle,
that tunnels through our ears, before it sews everything down, inside
the mind & heart, sitting at the apex of spirit,
where everything is calm, beauty coalesces inside touch,
the pianist hunches over his keyboard like a poet over his paper,
conjures up notes that burst sweet as cold purple grapes do
inside our mouths when they are perfectly ripe,
in season, the place green with spring or summer,
the music singing in & of itself, as fingers pull chords—
as poets pull words from someplace altogether mysterious—
in clusters that are seductive as language culled
from a place of magic, is where it all begins & ends now,
in this moment of clear seduction, the quiet is alchemized here,
is transformed by glorious sounds that are
enchanting as low purrs of lovers, their language cooing sweetness
as tongues wrapped, mysterious & bright as sunbeams teasing
touch here through slats of venetian blinds, this music clear as bars
of light slicing across shadows in a dark, dark room

II. ANTHONY DAVIS'S SET

the runs here remind me of balinese crystal geysers

spraying from waterfalls,
        here & there foaming into dissonance,
time signatures marching as time itself marches,
sound accumulating itself as it goes, car horns moving back & forth,
honking & blaring through traffic,
in manhattan, voices are also forms of accumulation,
the music here moving through space,
cutting like a razor but still
coasting, as order in chaos of times square moves through that time
as space mimicking motion but coasting anyway, revealing itself through speed
& quick change-up notions, the chameleon makeover artist there spiels
beyond what caution brings to any table
but up into symmetry anyway,
           is what it is all about here,
      nothing more or less than the sum total of rhythm,
what sound brings to our ears, our notion about the limits of artistry,
is what it is here, nothing less than energy
moving itself forward, or backward, or sideways like a sidewinder
rattlesnake, as black & white keys run disjunctive tension over themselves,
through themselves, hear everything mixed up as patois,
as mestizo, mulatto sounds, gumbo, jambalaya-american sounds
stewing in the black iron pot,
inside meltdown figures repeating themselves over & over again,
like trilling birds chirping somewhere deep inside forest-time are creating
deep magic, as in a choir of wolves mimicking thelonious monk,
their howls & yelps spraying foam as disjunctive syllables,
like after a headlong plunge through space & time a plume shaped
in the form of a feather tonguing out of the force of a waterfall hits rock,
creates music there that crescendos posthaste beyond any notion of modernity,
like deft speech does when it wears dark shades,
its words—"the bombs"—dressed up in neologic verbs & nouns
breaks into music, scats postbop like the pianist's hands bent here at the wrist,
curved fingers extended downward like long graceful necks of feeding swans,
turn into legs that tiptoe over keyboards like sleuths
moving through space with the beauty of bojangles robinson, & we watch
the pianist's fingers flashing over the black & white ivory keys in a blur,
hear the leapfrogging magic spewing mystery up into chords that echo

like birdcalls once heard in a munich english flower garden,
hear the ear-popping runs of art tatum here, the music transporting,
like a great meal washed down smooth with a great bottle of wine,
the moment here alchemistic, alcheringa, in the end, pure magic

## SYNCHRONICITY IN BOLOGNA, ITALY
*for Jeff Biggers & Bill Demby*


a sweet day strolling light here, breaking through breeze-licked
cool shadows, under terra-cotta porticoes, the sky up in the gables
streaked blue, where light plays off burnt sienna barriers that stand there
soft as moss clues in your eyeballs, as chewed-off red & ochre language flakes
here warm as bolognese spaghetti sauce, my sight leaps vertigo, all hues
held aloft here splash & dash through old walls all soft & warm too,
as caribbean seas lapping green-blue waters are filled with heat of lovers,
your eyeballs tongue honey-toned thighs of marvelously shaped women,
who are high-stepping it through these moments

                                        clear as church bells ringing
                                                  in the town

squares of hip bologna
            & we are seduced by the architecture here older than these words
sluicing through passageways, skirts of prancing young fine things flicking up
their switching beauty at the hemlines, reveal bodies
firmer than ripe grapes—& juicier, too—than sweet oranges on the vine—
hello—as they burst through time quicker than music heard here in castaneting
heels that bind the old to the bold, offered up as proof in footsteps that dance
behind you as we swivel our heads—readers—
catch a glimpse of a blur moving at the speed of sound & beauty,
mystery breaking through these moments like syllables flashing across
our view like saxophone, trumpet, or piano solos laced with silver, guitar sounds
breaking down here like jimi hendrix—& eye know it's all too hard to describe
or put together here, in a sentence—
how to appreciate it all, these glorious bodies swinging
like great solos jumping out of faces, dew-damp old buildings, doors,
what can be said but that they are marvelously sculptured clues racing through
the minds of those who live here now, or those like me, who are passing through,
who perhaps resemble this man, who looks like a sheep's eye of a bedouin,
who is passing me now might perhaps think americans cheap
& bittersweet as coca-colas,

his prickly black beard dusted with specks the color of cocaine,
his face serene as the truth george washington once told recounting cutting down
that mythical tree, the day here smelling of great food—as all the days here do —riding
a breeze that turns quickly on a dime—like a pirouette—it doubles back
to lick your face, coolly as you climb your spirit up the winding green road
that leads straight up to the top of the mountain,
a cool drink like a poem washing down your imagination,
                                                    roses & bougainvilleas
brightening up the tonguing, sweet air surrounding you,
as two rows of cypresses, straight as candle flames
                                        shoot skyward,
guard the road like sentries at the medieval castella de la romena,
south of bologna, in the appenini hills, where dante wrote
the thirty-first canto, north of vollombrosa
where milton wrote *paradise lost,*
                            above the devil's church,
where the monk fleeing the devil fell to his death screaming through
pure mountain air cold as a hawk diving down death on a prey,
on a day clear & perfumed as this one perhaps, as the valley rolls out below
like a rug full of patches of roasted barley & wheat,
their tops waving like elongated spiked heads of punk
rockers, in fields in sight of bartizans

& the old way of life rules supreme here still
outside of bologna, vollombrosa,
castella de la romena with its bartizan turrets, no plastic, or neon
culture ruling here, but architecture 800 years old,
& people carrying tradition in their moist olive eyes—

& who walk in a slow, measured gait in the countryside—

& where time is measured out by the number of breaths
one takes in, breathes out, afternoons wafting through lyrical here
as whispering flutes that become bassoons when dark fierce storms roll through,
their breath stabbed by cracking lightning bolts,

time leaving its mark on everything everywhere here,
in voices long gone but rustling still amongst trembling leaves of trees,
who speak to you during ghost moments after midnight,
speak to you too with joy, burnished as sienna walls

dusted with clues at the first crack of daybreak

# SIGHTING BIRDS AT THE BEACH

I. FLYING FISHERBIRDS
joined together behind the asshole nexus of a leader
two v-shaped lines of pelicans cruise overhead
in la jolla, winged fisherbirds headed out
into the boiling gray mist of a fog
foaming in from the pacific
on the downside of a
late but early
autumn
afternoon in
september, their cookie-
cutter bodies punching out irregular
black holes & shapes up there in space on a day
gray as sadness, these anglers gliding by like fighter planes
riding currents of wind & light, turning as they fly by in formation
their necks craning upward, straining outward—like wings slightly bent at
the tip—& downward (like cockpit cabins of concorde jets raising
lickety-split, hell-bent for europe) they rise up scanning
the rolling roiling waves, looking down beady-eyed
avengers scooping up fish from waving
water there—pelicans following
their spearheaded leader—
fisherbirds
tracking new skies
over boundless salt seas rancid
with the death-flesh odor of countless
entombed there—but a table of food stretching out
in front of a pelican's keen vision—wings spread wide to
catch a ride on sweet breaths of looping breezes there, totipalmates
webbed feet tucked underneath, like airplane wheels right after takeoff
their distensible pouch bills empty which drives them to dip
& glide ever alert eyes zeroing into curling waves for possible
kills, like heat-seeking radar one leaves the v-shaped
formation—knife blade plunging toward
the sea's heart—O pelican diving
O pelican—deep sea
fisherbird

## II. GRACEFUL SCAVENGERS

on the ground, seagulls wobble around beaches
like drunken, beady-eyed judges
without their black robes on, stepping stiff-legged across
sands dirty as the colors of their feathers
snatching food from the mouths of bawling toddlers
with their long, rapier-like beaks, they peck at beer cans,
styrofoam cups—anything they see, really—leaving webbed
birdprints tracking through sand, they look sideways out of mean
red eyes, wobbling about on toothpick legs, they wobble top-heavy
fat bodies around like black church deacons
or plump wall street executives, shuffling herky-jerky
side-to-side, their demeanor that of solemn funeral home directors
heads up, eyes alert for scraps of anything thought to be edible
their beaks jackhammering the earth as they strut by, gray-white
pilfering birds, so wretched down here on the ground
but lawd so beautiful cruising up there in space—
like anything the imagination thought was graceful or sleek—
easing in & out of wind currents, they bank & glide, float
& climb like a great idea spotlighted in prime time

MOTHER
*for Dorothy Smith Marshall*


when eye was growing up she used to sit in the bathroom, each & every
morning, smoking kool cigarettes, drinking hot coffee, reading newspapers,
a hard toilet seat caressing her derriere, reading glasses in place,
serious as cancer, the way her eyes devoured everything,
finished old newspapers stacked up high as her waistline when she stood
proud, erect, defiant, all of five feet two inches tall in high heel shoes, petite,
she was a pistol when she was young, eyes blazing, boring in
like bullets when her temper squeezed the trigger of her ire
hard, her rage angry scars she raised on me & my brother's backs & legs,
dealt out with ironing cords that hissed through the air like whips, coiled snakes
about to strike, it was her mother's influence (she was scared to death of her
mother—mama to me & my brother timmy—), who believed in retribution,
payback, fear, to the bitter end we watched mama slap mother around hard,
once or twice, for some perceived transgression, or indiscretion,
but we loved them both deeper than fear itself,
loved mother, mama too, because we knew we were a lot to handle—
my brother & me—born to do mischief in a neighborhood full of young thieves,
malcontents, murderers-to-be, you name it, they thrived & flourished there—
the good & straight we rejected out of hand as past tense, negro, square
as blocks we played with once until we wrapped hands around straight razors—
so she cracked the whip hard, raised welts on our backs & hardening butts,
legs & arms, kept fear alive in us, to keep us in line, & alive

she always had books around the house, introduced me to poetry & novels,
wanted to be a schoolteacher, raising me & my brother got in the way of that
& as she grew older she left a string of glassy-eyed suitors
in her wake, my father being the first who didn't make it all the way
home, where her sweet perfume trailed through the air like flowers
blooming fresh in springtime, gardenias of lady day, sometimes
jasmine, or roses, it depended on her mood, but there was always something
about her that kept them coming back for more, time & again,
whatever she had bewitched them with, her charm, maybe,
that could be as dazzling as the smile flashing above her sensuous walk

{ *277* }

that beckoned, her step so light she seemed to float through air, meriny-yellow
in skin tone, plum, cushiony lips, splashed bright red & full, smooth,
she called herself a party girl—though she was always much more than this,
though she was this, too—with a great sense of style, dressed to kill cock-
robin, could press pedal to the metal out on the dance floor,
she caused heads to swivel on necks like spinning tops,
whenever she passed, her fragrance tantalizing nostrils,
trailing behind her like a sweet-smelling, invisible plume

she's in her eighties now, still sits on the toilet stool each & every morning,
repeating the same ritual, only now she doesn't smoke anymore,
everybody's gone to the other side on her side of the family—mama,
her brothers garfield & allen, aunts & uncles, cousins, her daddy, mine too—
men her age still sniff behind her glassy-eyed, whenever she honors them
when she looks their way, still a fashion plate, the best of her time, her smile
remains dazzling, her skill to squeeze copper from a penny, squirrel away
money—a survivor of the depression, she is tenacious—for rainy days,
she's softer now, tells me she loves me every time we speak
over the telephone, tells me, with regret, she could have done better by me,
but that's hogwash, because she did the best she could with what she had,
& that was more than enough to get us through all the madness,
she is still a pistol at 81, has all of her real teeth, too, has outlived all her
suitors, except this last one, biff, who, she says, is slowing down at 79,
she still walks with a bounce in her stride, seems to still float across
& through the air, her eyes blazing bore in on you still like bullets
whenever she squeezes the trigger of her hot temper, ire
& eye love her more than eye could ever imagine,
love her far deeper than fear itself

# JEREZ DE LA FRONTERA
*for Peter*

I.

in the deep black hours of jerez, after midnight, margaret is a mummy
wrapped in a white sheet where she sleeps, in the dead of night, she lies
in the center of our bed, stiff as demeanors of some european aristocrats, peter,
your house quiet as church mice sniffing gold leaf pages of a book of sacrament,
a cool breeze licking in over white walls & slanted roofs from the east filters
heat, announces morning light is not far off, wedded, as it is, to daybreak, soon
the white bridal gown of first light will spread out its hem, lift its white lace
veil, while a lengthening train of clues breaks the dark into spreading
blues, which are current everywhere, common as the lyrics of muddy waters,
john lee hooker, lightnin' hopkins, somewhere deep inside
a snoring voice of lament breaks through the last vestiges of quiet hours,
at the center of a slippery moment full of dreaming, a motorbike zips through,
leaning around corners, it escalates the language of its speed as it shoots, veers,
clues itself into somewhere it is due, gearing down toward silence as it blows
past white walls & roofs collaged in bold relief against a spangled black sky,
they look like still lifes from my second-floor window over the garden,
while margaret's sweet fragrance rises like seduction from where she sleeps,
her body a stand-in for a mummy wrapped in white linen, her face sweet,
is turned toward the window as if to kiss first light when it comes

II.

now a sliver of moon smiles through our room above the tiny chimneys,
they seem to wear small hats cocked ace-deuce, like the icon of tio pepe sherry,
peter has told us of the burning hot wind of dust & fire called la vente,
which brings grief from the east, when the weather vane's arrow head points
in the direction of seville, granada's alhambra, lorca's moorish part of andalusia,
its craggy mountain peaks sharp as alligator teeth, their skin the color of chalk
brown mixed with ochre, greens, reds, white villages & towns—
& one the shape of one of miró's floating birds—sweep across this heat-
stricken landscape of late august, up & down rolling, warbled landscapes,
rendered mysterious by el greco's surreal, strangely beautiful canvases,
they seem to be rising up from some moonscape, somber dream,

but today the weather vane arrows north, toward madrid & morning
breaks through smells of coffee, footsteps that crack hard as castanets, or skulls
being popped open when smashed against old cobblestone streets, spilled brandy
that stained tiled squares checkerboarding the walkway of the plaza plateros
last night, is being washed clean, right before daylight breaks apart my dreams,
eye hear in the center of my imagination the roar of a bullring, erupting
cheers in the arena roll up & down, a cadence of emotive conundrum,
& in the middle of it all eye feel the matador slaying the bull,
in the center of the arena, see its blood flowing bright as the matador's red suit,
emblazoned with golden epaulets, hear in my mind's ear clapping castanets,
cracking sounds of flamenco dancers shoes slapping the floor staccato,
in a rhythm reminding me of popping sounds of conga drums, miles' lamenting
trumpet on *Sketches of Spain,* now that the sun is high in the blue eye follow
the curve of his mournful lament, fully awake now, walk down
to your walled-in courtyard peter, bright with green, yellow chumbera cactus
buds, bright birds of paradise shoot out blooming tongues that burst into heads,
geraniums fragrant as the sparkling water fountain is lyrical, tantalize
the senses, you want to sit here forever amongst these red & yellow lobster
claws, scarlet red begonias laddering, emblazoning these old walls,
want to sit & write poems of hope & serenity, but today, back in the states,
president clinton is being deposed in front of a grand jury, people screaming
his head be axed off, thrown into a bucket like fish, or snakes

but you wring out words of joy, peter, they roll off your tongue lyrical
as a happy mantra, relieved the weather vane's arrowhead still points north,
the breeze tongue cool as springs of water high in mountains of italy,
you are relieved the day is not scorching hot with la vente,
though we hear words circling the american congress like declarations of war,
on that day we would go down to the beach between cádiz & rota,
where the waves washing in rough & warm were beautiful, the sun setting low,
in the west, just before evening wrapped itself around us like the arms
of a favorite relative, my spirit reaching out across the straits of gibraltar felt
the tip of africa, so close, so far away, the promontory of cádiz pointing
like a finger full of white buildings toward the dark continent,
when the light grew dark as the sun dropped like a ripe orange into the sea,
where ships crawled into port like giant bugs, sea gulls glided over & through
the sweet, cool air, like toy planes banking over waves thick as molasses,

the air here thick with andalusian spanish, syllables cracking rapid fire,
machine-gun staccato, the laughter sudden as terrorist explosions,
spontaneous as great music is always, everywhere it is played

III.

night has come again to this place of caballos, noble horses & brave fighting
bulls with curved horns trying to kill a matador with a red cape,
toro, toro, toro, bravo, toro, the cheers rise as the bloody black bull charges,
toro, toro, toro, a man & a red cape & a horse, the spectacle beyond what
eye feel is beauty, though eye see there in movement the sheer power,
choreography of war, the grace of man & beast during a moment
at the edge of death, locked into a mode of survival, is as far as my heart can go
in the service of destruction for beauty, who am eye to say what is or isn't glory,
the lance poised in the air like a scorpion's tail before the strike is art for so many,
murder to others, in this land of the inquisition & franco's execution of lorca,
what is there to know but your own heartbeat pulsing love, peter,
the blood of friendship pure as your smile or hug, these bodegas of wine you have shared
peter, full of the finest sherry, meals scarfed down & laughter shattering moments
like gunfire, these are the things you remember, castanets & flamenco dancers,
the chimneys cocked ace-deuce like icons of tio pepe in the cool evenings,
your gracious, spontaneous smile, my friend, your friendship brought us here,
for me to see margaret's body wrapped like a mummy in lacy white linen,
asleep in the center of our bed, the shades open, in the dead of fragrant nights,
her face sweet, always turned toward the open window, as if to kiss
the first morning light when it comes, is a blessing & a gift,
eye tell you now, peter, it is a blessing & a rare, poetic gift

THE POINT LOMA POEMS:
WRITTEN FOR THE WASTEWATER MANAGEMENT PROJECT
*for the Sculptor, Mathieu Gregoire, who got me involved*


I.
reader, let your painterly imagination run true as a brushstroke,
straight out to sea, let your eyes zoom along a single line
curving away from this artificial walkway & barrier,
this cliff of sand, clumps of grass, large & small boulders, look
out toward the horizon, where blue meets blue on a clear day,
where a bar of mist separates the two, the view expansive everywhere
from here, the blue sky spreading soft lips of air to kiss the many
feverish mouths of fish opening & closing out in the pacific,
where desire is a need to hold all this power in check,

where that straight line you pull yourself out by now holds true,
on course, your eyes drinking in everything your mind can swallow,
there, where the mouth that holds the tongue that speaks
in breaking syllables, with foaming articulation, roaring in in one curling wave
after another, suds at the point of apogee, like a madman stunned by a miracle
when he looks out, sees a single color between green & violet meet
each other as lovers fuse at the point where the sun touches their flesh,
at each place along their line of connection, we are fascinated by it all,
when light fades toward alchemy, the power deeply magical here,
mysterious as touch when it seduces flesh, where true colors fade into gradual
gradations, the palette swelling with cool heat of blues where your vision leaps
out now reader, to embrace the glow that holds the line
true from this point forward, now

reach out your ears & senses toward titillation, stretch them out,
listen to, feel the music re-creating itself out there where the sun refracts
its lancing rays that multiply into a billion slivers of light that cut
& sparkle like diamonds on the back of this blue ocean, a miracle
spread out like an endless azure veranda (table toward which pelicans & sea-
gulls dive, swoop over & feed on squawking & barking like hungry sea lions
everywhere on wet, black rocks), the language of a poem that suddenly grows

wings, takes off in flight, reaches this place here where sea, land, & sky meet
light, at the end of point loma, beneath a slope of scrub bush, bright magenta
ice plants & pickle, now let your mind rest here, space traveler,
where weeds climb these hillsides of green & rough brown
rocks—now a grave from where four dooky flames used to shoot
orange lizard tongues rippling skyward, miraging air with heat,
waves that whales use to navigate themselves in by,
after crossing the pacific, geysering up spray foam jets from holes
in their backs, drench with saltwater where waves curl, form patterns
way out in the humping mad waves locked like lovers,
waves moving up & down like a chain of U's, curving question marks, way up
above poseidon holding his three-pronged fork, who can cause earthquakes
to lift the towering water higher until it breaks & dives down smashing
against the surface/skin, it becomes a boiling cauldron there,

imagine yourself in that boiling cauldron of curling power, reader,
a whale or a surfer or eyes from a boat looking back at this stunning
land, rising as if it were the outer walls of a bowl seen from here as a backdrop,
the sea floor curving up to meet it, form the highest rim, imagine stunned reader,
it is the golden hour of seven in the evening, you are riding a wave in,
it's summer & a bar of sunlight wrinkles & ripples across the surface of waves
as they wash in before disintegrating as foam on the shining black rocks,
now imagine this: you are a surfer & the same ray of sunlight behind your head
casts a light that reflects off your surfboard onto the waves,
you think you're looking into a mirror, then a halo circles around
your body as you ride the imploding power cruising toward extinction,

look now & see the vortex, reader, swelling around rocks before you
like rings around jupiter, where brown kelp swims tangled as nests of snakes
inside tidepools, swirling inside mouths of yawning caves next to wet black
rock islands holding shimmering seals
washed bright as black babies' shiny bottoms, wet with pee,
the air here smelling of salt, waves crashing in carrying the power
& language of tornadoes howling like runaway trains,
still there is a feeling of calmness where you stand looking out through
pelting mist, waves slobbering fringes of lace exhaust themselves
like madmen in eddying, swirling shapes,
in this tide pool where you stand just now, reader, you are

following these words to the land's end to watch them disappear,
only to appear somewhere else, perhaps right around the corner,
like waves & currents at the end of another journey

II.

& now you find yourself back here again before your eyes
& mind began to roam, again, before you imagined yourself out there
in all that power looking in, the air here smelling of bromide,
mixed with the sharp odor of garbage,
now you stand here again reading these lines
before moving down the granite path parallel to the tide pool, the land's end
& wherever you go now the smell of humankind is everywhere—
after all, each san diegan leaves a little piece of themselves
out here, a piece of memory, soiled plastic gloves, condoms, chewing gum,
their wrappers glinting in kidneys of pulverized dogs, smashed tin cans,
some leftover potatoes gone to goo, a lost diamond ring, perhaps,
a coin swirled down a toilet stool with that stinking eel-like long stuff that slides
soft as a snake from someone's derriere, a blitzkrieg of snails crushed beyond
whatever your recognition can handle, after a rainstorm, something
sharp as a blade of glass, a steel pitcher, a crab, a seashell,
a cornucopia of anything imaginable ends up out here—
at the end of point loma, gathered in a truly democratic state,
inside lakes full of ferric chloride, anionic polymer,
inside gigantic sed-tanks armed with aluminum teeth,
all carried here by cutthroat or parsifal flumes
that separate liquids from solids that fall to the bottom of tanks,
there to be scraped to one end to become sludge matter
pumped into digestors, it is cooked as food is inside stomachs,
turned into gases & transformed into electricity that runs everything
here on point loma, the liquid pumped through rainbows of underground pipes,
sluicing & rushing with the sound of pulverizing floods, it zooms itself out
through dusty tunnels of concrete & steel, is shot out
quick as a blink into the pacific,
shot way out through a gigantic high-powered gun,
whose trigger is forever being pulled

III.

wastewater becomes a tongue of speech that commingles
inside that dark shadowy world where denizens of the deep
sleep, where life is cold & cheap & heights & depths are sheer
& steep, where long-lost secrets keep cold in heaps of stones, rest
side by side with bones, where above it all, in the brimming sunlight,
swimmers & dolphins skim, break the surface carried by waves,
where you see yourself now, reader & traveler, memorizing a place
where you throw your vision out to again, somewhere,
at the point where sea meets sky, the color there somewhere in between
green & violet, a warm sun touching that place with affection,
as in the seduction you, too, feel now, when you allow your mind to open
as a flower grown here in this barren place of great beauty, bloom,
like life anywhere breath is taken, the moment here cherished,
embraced as creation shaped by love, what it is before you now,
here, at the land's end, the color somewhere in between
green & violet, where the sea meets the sky,
where the sea is married to the sky

IV.

a long winding road takes you away from this place
of humming machines & low concrete buildings,
side by side with hot pink bougainvilleas, slow sounds of men
pile-driving stones in hard hats below chattering helicopters
hovering in patrol just off shore, at the land's end, danger in high
voltage wires popping & snapping warning signs everywhere,
hissing messages in black lettering against canary yellow, chipped black
on white, beige against brown, a mirror checking you out as you pass,
everywhere dusted with fine chalk here,
a kind of institutional sameness, now leave all that behind
& move out down this snaking path, pass a parking lot out beyond the hum
of men & machines struggling to leave their mark on destiny & control,
where the land ends, forms the head of a sea otter,
its body the cliff wall falling away to the rocks below, where
waves crash spending their hissing language of frilly lace,
like breath of people back out in the real world,
the beauty of this place & the sea stretching out here

in front of your eyes, your imagination carrying you
anywhere you want to, on a gray day even, cuddling inside
the sweetness of your lover's almond-shaped eyes that speak to you
now, so seductively here, inside your head when that voice whispers
your name sweet as anything you could ever imagine,

so smile when you think of love blooming as a flower,
watching the freedom of a seagull soaring above everything,
these walls where you can read these words, come closer,
don't ever be afraid of these words,
come closer, rub your mind up against them as you stroll this path,
turn them over like they are good food inside your brain,
chew on them, treat them as if they were long-lost friends come back
to visit you, here, dropped in from anywhere,
they won't hurt you, now watch them as they move as flight,
as birds spreading wings & climbing skyward,
across the pages of your mind,
toward the sun, think of them as freedom, my friend,
as sprung from a dream, the future in this seagull
perched on this wall hit by sunlight,
think of these words as guides, new-found friends
as you walk out in all this glorious air & light here,
feel the wind's tongue rubbing up against your scrubbed face,
the music of the waves crashing & roaring like a lover's climax
when they hit rocks & you'll know freedom there,
rough & cold & late, but still beautiful,
yes, think of these words as keys to freedom my friend,
syllables that are keys unlocking doorways to freedom,
that lead you along this north nature path,
yes, think of them as freedom, friend,
savor these words here at the land's end,
that is shaped like a sea otter's head

    v.

& the sea otter's head connects the path that leads us
up the backside of this windswept place, the path winding
higher & higher, swinging up & bending around

this barren spot like an elongated L, or a boomerang slicing
behind eight digestors that serve as stomachs,
scrub brush squatting on hillsides sloping up or down—
whatever your perspective—thorn bushes
wedged into rock & dirt, wind & birds waltzing at your back
disguised as mozart or bach, what you hear inside your head now
is what you evoke there hiking this east slope nature path,
the rim of the hill above you quilting
colors of various browns & greens, beethoven's music
playing dramatic in the thundering swells bursting against rocks,
& when you look out at the pacific from here you can see
beyond what you saw before when you were down there,
amongst the low sounds of electricity humming, mixed with jackhammering,
hard-hatted men (who probably listen to music of elvis or country & western—
maybe you, too, reader, or perhaps miles davis, tupac shakur,
duke ellington, or U2), your mind running out in front of you now,
or resting in meditation, awestruck by what you see out in all that blue,
the view stretching out from yourself to embrace the humpback
coronado islands off of baja, planes arrowing skyward from lindbergh field,
helicopters split in half by rays of light from the sun, clouds cruising away fast
as some promises made by politicians, on a clear day

the possibility of seduction by what you see here is everywhere
around you, as you trip the light fandango, play off
the waves that dance & swell, you hear the sound of castanets
in your head, see the licking light moving up the magenta slope
as the sun goes down, click by click, as if it were measured by a clock
inside God's head, the movement now from bright glare
to lengthening shadows with every click,
& with every click waves climb higher up walls,
leave seashells in tidewater basins looking like white skulls
from here, as the sun drops golden, click by click, its legacy is its light
reaching out a long orange arm across the darkening water to touch
you here, reader, where you stand or move along & through
this pathway of rock & gravel, this thicket of turning pages,
below the rim of this hill time stretching out before you now
(an act of possibility or love?), as the sky turns orange-

gold, just before twilight, you embrace beauty where you are
reader, embrace the highest possibility of yourself, right now,
at this moment, embrace the parameters of an idea,
whose time has come, is singing here, right now

# THE POINT LOMA SERIES OF HAIKUS & TANKAS

*for Mathieu Gregoire*

I.

beauty all places
here, look inside yourself now,
look deeper, it's there

II.

gray day underground
in the tunnel, bright, warm sun
outside in the blue,
inside your own deep working
time, thoughts of making sweet love

III.

think of making love
to the work that you do here,
think of it as song,
music whispering, a breeze,
a tongue of someone you love

IV.

think of a sweet place,
now that you are here, in all
this darkness, light where
you are standing with yourself,
wherever you have to go

V.

smile whenever you
think of the sweet love blooming
inside your hard head,
think of it as a flower
you will hand to someone soon

VI.
down here in darkness
think of roses when you look
at these concrete walls

VII.
your mind a window
to look inside yourself, see
a rich garden there,
bright with flowers, whose faces
pop the air like sweet music

VIII.
deep rumblings in air,
is sound of sea waves smashing
skulls of wet black rocks

IX.
somewhere on a hill
burning candle flames—tall pines
shoot up, reach skyward,
their v, for victory, signs—
lick hot tongues, scorch the air

## YOUR LOVER'S EYES SPEAK

your lover's eyes speak
to you so softly in this
place of wind, sea, bright blue sky,
sunlight after the gray lifts,
stuns your face into smiling

## COME CLOSER

come closer, don't be afraid of these words,
come closer, rub your mind up against them,
see in them the possibility that birds seek,
like ones perched on the other side of this wall
& further out to see where the waves crash,
aren't they beautiful there dressed all in black
& white feathers, like some skin-tones, look, see
them in their flocks there in the sun shaking off
water sprays from their feathers, now their wings
opening & closing before they take flight to freedom,
as sea waves crash in in foaming thunder leaving
their lace hissing at the top of their curling flight,
crashing, then eddying back out as spent bubbles,
look at all this evoked in the words of this poem,
isn't it beautiful, the view seen from here
my friend, on this dark wall leading up
to snatch a little sunlight at the end of this
tunnel, my friend, dig down & find the light
within yourself, see that seagull there ready
to take flight, as if sprung from a dream, there
as you walk out this dark tunnel into the glorious
air & light, you hear waves crashing their thunder
as the seagull takes flight, you know freedom's
out there, at the end of these words

# BROKEN IN PARTS:
## A HEALING SONG FOR SAXOPHONE & VOICE
*for Oliver Lake & Kwame Ture (Stokely Carmichael) 1941–1998*


I.

broken in parts, broken in parts, the earth fractured & fissured
is broken in parts, voices censored, broken off in space,
in their place the silent ooze of breathing, pulsating between worlds
between place parts of syntax floating on surfaces of speech like islands
floating in the middle of rivers, in the middle of nowhere & everywhere
    zigzagging omens waving flags of menace like flapping tongues,
everything seemingly coming apart in a sea of wreckage,
someone is drowning we don't hear or see,
threads suddenly gone, clues, beliefs
suddenly torn asunder by sawblading teeth, hemorrhaging
blue-meanies shooting through dreams after winds blew buzz saw glass
through dazed wonder, life chewed up between jackhammering jaws,
as a razor cuts through a living tongue & it is bleeding
speech cannot form itself again around words,
when language we once knew but now hear as garbled

is broken in parts, broken in parts, language fractured & fissured,
                                      broken in parts


II.

what to do then, when men and women cannot speak,
when meaning is sawed off clean & language becomes a chimney chute
through which sound sweeps as ash coating everything with a sooty pallor,
before syllables can form in the cave of the spirit that issues words, cadences,
that used to roll out like musical notes off the sweetness tongues suddenly cut
clean to blooming silence, dumb screams there now, oozing blood,
where the silver steel flashed red underneath halloween street lamps,
flies swarming around a gaggle of slit throats

& in the middle of it all a chewed up black pencil of a man,
who stands holding his tongue between his hands,

                              silence surrounding him like a mourning shawl,
& what is the belief holding up his laddering backbone there,

the tongue in his hands now was once a saxophone when whole,
was a blur of fingers whooshing through golden keys of his voice belling
like charlie parker burning riffs quick as michael johnson cruising
solo, lickety-split, his turbo-driven voice used to turn flips,
somersaults, turn around in midair like great olympic figure skaters,
their bodies doing twists, the moment there alive, fused
with magic, probed limits of the tongue, unpredictable as mystery,
it once moved to re-create itself, again & again, through improvisation,
sought to push the edge of its creation out beyond boundaries of what
anything would allow, the vocabulary flowing back & forth,
like a mantra, before silence cut through
its song, turned it into ripples on the surface of a river, gone
after a rock dropped through its shimmering, wet skin, through a vortex,
where the eye now catches a language of shadows, once lengthening,
now they are breaking apart in waves of fragmentation

    III.
but we can speak with our eyes, can fashion them into a tongue,
can turn that tongue into a living voice that conjures up song,
conjures up spirits, the drumbeat of strong hearts goosing everything along,
like a great drummer keeping time, evenly kept, pulsating breath, strong,
sluicing through the tempo of the lungs,
through death we can travel backward to ancestors through our spirits,
through our mind's juju, we can go down to the station of resurrection,
wait for the underground train marked with vèvès to arrive there,
we can board that train, dream ourselves into magic through imagination,
can walk inside history longside power sleeping deep down inside us, now,
deeper still, deeper than the limits of fear ever allowed us to travel,
because our black cat's bone knows the mojo spirit is listening,
knows the mojo bone can rest in our hands if we dream ourselves deeper,
deep enough to dream ourselves into beauty, deeper still, go down deeper,
deeper, so we can conjure up the power of a black mojo hand,
deeper, so we can restore speech to a severed tongue cut off in a storm
by buzz saw slivers of glass propelled through the dark,

by the awesome power of a tornado's wind,
or cut off by evil, unhuman men, who think love is a gun, a bloody knife
salvation, we can conjure up the power of a black mojo hand, can reconnect
flesh with flesh, expression, can beat human madness with our own magic,
voodoo, can reconnect these islands of words floating through broken
sentences, fractured & fissured, broken apart,
words floating like drowned faces bloated after a sudden flood brought death,
we can reconnect these words & fashion a language out of silence, space,
a language of fragments that can float in the air like chords,
echoing the music of monk's genius, miles, we can hear it if we listen,
can feel it if we listen, can reconnect that pencil-thin black man's tongue,
once a saxophone's voice, can stitch that voice back together again into song,
into music again with a needle stitching love, can weave magic
fashioned there out the bone of a mojo-hand,
can put it all back together again if we listen & feel love,
sluicing poetry & voodoo out of a mojo hand singing through a tongue rooted
                                              within the spirit of healing,
magic & mystery, the song becoming beauty, so listen to beauty
beating in your own human hearts, listen to the healing
powers fashioned from bone of our own mojo hand
& beating in our own singular hearts


    IV.
& the music is jabber-walking across space & air
& comes whispering
& whispering comes carrying
the burden of silence with it for so very long,
beyond this whispering of echoes,
a wish to reconnect this language, this tongue broken in parts,
broken articulation, beliefs, clues, broken into islands of words,
phrases, isolated beyond meaning, now
silence breaking into sound that is guttural, blues seeded,
inside timbre of the voice rising now to form some kind of language,
reaching for beauty, trying to unify fragments
into complete sentences,
though broken apart now it is trying to coalesce,
come back together again, for love,

for beauty, for family, so listen
for words floating up from the abyss into recognizable sound that evokes
familiar faces, that are pulled out of a raging, flooded river,
see recognition now in those blinking eyes,
magic unfolding in language rising up there guttural but pure,
reborn here as tongue restored, reconnected
speech returned to voice
inside the mouth,
words form, roll off the tongue,
carry faces carved from history,
faces that string themselves together to fashion a memory,
a memory that is a necklace of love beads draped around our necks,
imagine those faces as metaphors now, seeds
for love songs whispering,
tonguing just outside your ear,
imagine those words as possible healing powers,
a healing love song, whispering now,
whispering, inside your ear


    v.

language is rolling off the tongue now.
acril le la, cra cra, acril le la, ah booka sonday, listen,
the song sings, the bird/man sings way up above the blue,
above the blues, but rooted in those funky dues,
miles playing the blues while the wind is sleeping deep down inside
his blue trumpet, voice, the sound haunting
deep down inside the blues, ah booka sonday,


the wind grows deeper in thunder,
the day puts on its clothing of golden laughter,
wearing its golden flames up there in the blue, travels around spring-
time sewing bright green manes, everywhere, sewing sweet magic back
into the breath, stitched through a voice of blue mystery, is your tongue,
your cockadoodle do, soukas turning flips inside your ears,
is your gin & tonic blues, universal diva,

wearing a deep blue dress any day, a flower in her hair
like lady day singing "strange fruit,"
these are the songs forming in the throat

these are the songs, ah booka sonday

VI.
& these songs are you turned inside out,
your tongue reconnected now, your voice yourself,
echoing you resurrected, your words carrying faces
you pulled from the river of memory,
from the blood of your own healing your language comes

                                                     fusing longing & love

& kisses the day now dressed in blue & green & light,
kisses the day now dressed in who-do-you-love, flight,
the bird/man singing through you

from way up above the blues, above the light,
the distance traveled from him to you now, a clue unlocking
golden traces of solos, pulsating light,

& miles is a moonshot covering the musical distance

from your own heartbeat to this solo, speaking here,
your own language zipping through as pure sound, zigzagging
lightning bolts zipping up the night, is your own solo here riffing,
acril le la, cra cra, acril le la,

sound, beat, thumping through your own voice,
creating inside the drumbeat of your own heart,

& it is you singing now, as a poet,

is your own reconnected tongue, singing

# BELLS
*after Gustaf Sobin*


eye am hearing bells in the music of poetry, bells
inside laughter tinkling like silver, bells rinsed in colors, shapes
& forms washing wave after sonorous wave, bells washed through
wind chimes, swept through morning's first breaking light, rolling
bells shivering in damp cool speech hip language seduces
& imitates, bells coursing through syllables spilling from lips,
bells tinkling through raindrops, pooling on rooftops,
spreading like rosebuds, airborne on wind tongues,
drooling down storm drains, riding water through whirlpools,
drop by dropping drop, bells spooling electric
through hearts in sacred himalayan mountains of tibetan buddhists, bells
swirling through pooling deep eyes of lovers, trilling inside bright voices
raised by small children, bells seducing through winds that play games
with our minds, with the way we hear time slipping through our ears,
& there are bells heard in kisses when sucking lips meet, vibrating,
electric bells, strolling bells, breeze-blown that tongue
through fragrant afternoons of spring/time,
bells in silver dewdrops shimmying down bright green leaves
that land & float like rafts skimming surfaces of glass-blue rivers,
bells that dive through sparkling waterfalls like voices or solos
rinsed with clear welling sounds that tickle our senses
like crystal runs of bill evans laying down clues, bells sluicing through,
in flight, the way a thief steals through the night's deep music like a sleuth,
the way blues tiptoes over piano keys dropping bell notes here
& there as chords shimmy-shangling through the thick night air rinsed
in shimmering, electric beauty, bells that render us spellbound,
as when the heart seduces sound by locking up pure
rhythm that is light, conjuring bells that speak in voices dazzling,
church bells that ring inside seductive sweet strides of dancing women,
as when bells roll through their hips swaying lyrical, incredible magic, & eye
heard bells in heat of summer language making sweet flowers rise,
heard bells in the voice of pavarotti's "nessun dorma,"
heard bells clanging & rolling through the square fronting westminster abbey,

heard bells in the sound of african dew mornings rising, trumpets blaring,
heard bells in the silver ice of hale-bopp's streaking comet tail,
heard bells ringing throughout plazas of freedom everywhere—
but not from the cracked fluke bell squatting mute in philadelphia—
heard bells inside all beauty heard or seen anywhere,
bells, bells, splendid sweet bells,
heard bells in the seduction of great poetry singing,
heard bells ringing through the luminous language of sweet birds
riffing, bells, bells, splendid sweet bells,
swelling inside the air's sweet music

CHORUSES

*for Allen Ginsberg, 1926–1997, and Lucy Goldman*


1.

within the muted flight of daybreak, inside its leaked, trembling light
of birth, after the cracked shell of night's dome has split open,
cut loose a flurry of pitched voices grown from different, linguistic sperm,
we hear a cacophony of opposing rhythms integrated inside the body of a song,
carried as if upon the widespread feathered wings of a bird across the sky
of imagination, as in the circling, beating mantra the heart knows
as breath becoming choruses, becoming soundtracks
lifted off a poet's chanting tongue, syllables become moments
within moments, are transformed into song
beautiful as any morning glory colors when the sun slants down,
cuts through whatever is there with its golden blades, becomes beams
bright & sharp as voices heard anywhere hands meet drumheads of skin
tightly pulled, the rhythms vibrating there in skimming waves
washing in or out at you as if they were imitating foaming sound rolling in from
the sea, curling tips of its waves into shape of grigri lips that can be cataclysmic
as foam sudsing off lips of madmen moaning, or roaring,
or doing whatever it is madmen do, in katmandu, in the center
of nepal, or on the streets of new york city, where voices fire up pitches
fast as old satchel paige threw a baseball down the heart of the plate
or snaked it across inside or outside corners disguised as an aspirin,
like sound nicks away edges of language, chips off syllables & meaning,
until the voice cracks words electric as static,
perhaps resembles the sound lightning bolts make when ripping off small pieces
    of dark sky & space
when thunder cracks its jagged whip across the night's high gloom

there, where wolves sing love songs to the moon, where lookeloos crane
their necks on freeways trying to spot hale-bopp comet's streaking silver ice tail,
who listen to songs of beck over the radio hightailing it lickety-split through
this dark out west, burning rubber signatures into asphalt, as cars
wheel in & out of traffic, screech brakes, shape a kind of music, a new language
only the initiate know & imitate as it twists itself around again & again,

{ *300* }

doubles-back in the way rhythm turns in & back on itself,
like a concrete pretzel claiming its own place as it curls into space,
lifts off in the shape of interwoven, interlocking freeway ribbons carrying cars
& speech above our heads on conveyer belts as motors screaming high speed
octane, zooming around curves like crazed vagabonds
hitting moments of sweet need, as music fills the air with magical incantations
wrapped in voices that track down sound, then double back blue as terror
recycles itself through years when good old boys guzzled beers
on back roads of america in a slew of cars that sped down roads twisted as limbs
of people suffering from rheumatoid arthritis, gunracks over their faces,
grinning like cheshire cats who just ate a slew of canary birds,
yellow feathers scattered all over that sordid history
& everywhere blood on whiskers of hyenas, blood frozen in ice-
cold stares of serial killers, blood in drawing rooms of politicians practicing
blood sports, bullshitting us in washington, blood on the cheese face of a leering
moon after eclipse hung down over rancho santa fe, blood on grimacing faces
bursting from bloated black bodies in rwanda, blood exploding from that
incinerated house in waco, texas, blood shooting from the eyes of a child before
he pulled the trigger in paducah, kentucky, blood in the speeches of ministers
pontificating from pulpits, blood all up in the curdling screams sliced clean
through by razors, blood smeared all over the blues
choruses of screams heard chilling after explosions in jerusalem,
in the choruses of hand grenades tattooing the nights of bulgaria, colombia,
in the choruses of machine gun bursts stitching the evenings of mexico city,
los angeles, that snuffed out the life of notorious b.i.g., tupac in las vegas,
choruses of fire meeting choruses of bullets, choruses of hand grenades
greeting the imploding language of love, blood on the syllables, choruses
spewing blood on musical notes that sing of these times everywhere

& blood on money pulled from ocean bottoms by deep-sea divers,
blood up in the voices of poets impregnating stanzas with music,
blood on tongues cut off because they sang beautiful images of love,
blood where the land mines littered the earth with eyeballs,
skulls, & severed hands that point accusatory fingers stiff as bones in the mud,
& choruses & blood & choruses & blood, choruses & blood,

behold the time-clocks ticking inside blood irrigating flesh,
inside the moment when the poet knows language as a wellspring,
inside the moment when truth is understood as a two-headed sword
duplicitous as the notion there is true beauty in flesh, lyrical with movement,
final as death, time marches on, leaves' flesh imprinted with maps of spiderweb
sites, that spread across the body's internet, as songs pealing across
this embezzled air tantalize us with history of our continued failure

II.
when we sing we hear & know the music best, hear it with hearts
imitating breath, the rhythm of drumbeats in cadences
true poets hear, the heartbeat of their breath in time signatures spread,
scored like music across fleet pages scrolling the mind, dreams composed within
language, when words become musical notes or chords, language is traced back
where it first burst from song as anchored root,
grew into a melody (a sweet flower smelled in springtime,
summer, when birds clear their throats of seeds, open piccolo beaks
& run tremolos beautiful, at dizzy gillespie speed)

& there is joy in the sweet singing of melodies,
beauty in the voice marveling at the sweet, blessed curves of a lover's
ripe body, in the way a woman's mind is shaped, her thighs, breasts, her lips
caressing in the way a dress might caress the sensuousness of her body,
pure joy in the rapture of her kiss, blood boiling over there with sweet heat,
glory in her song, glory in the choruses of blood singing
beneath her flesh, choruses of heartbeats drumming faster & faster still,
glory in the mind running over from a space rooted in love,
where a poet creates from inside a moment of stillness, silence,
when metaphor is ejaculated from mystery into language,
sluices from the brain as words scaffolded onto the page like archipelagos
strung out in a sea of air like notes blown complete from a bell of a trumpet,
becomes poetry when form connects structure with magic, when breath
carries poetry with the indelible smell of damp rooms after lovemaking,
rumpled sheets stained with semen, history, the claustrophobic odor of cigarettes
when jamming their crooked, burnt-out butts into overflowing ashtrays,
into rooms drenched with stale smell of whiskey & garbage
& all this forms a question mark, a gesture—

a hand curved in space & bent at the wrist—a fragrance of mystery evoking
the color of pastel drenched with lilting speech of the caribbean hinting of soft
seas, the air there filled, fragrant with garlic, peanut oil, saffron,
orange-gold sunsets laced with magenta, pink streaked with magical coral
reefs, purple threaded like veins through blue, the feel of it is a chorus,
is a song lifted from the blood of the sky by a poet who sings
another prayer at sunset, practices ancient science of cabala,
cabala lore, cabala, cabala lore, cabala

III.

& eye heard you passed away today allen ginsberg, heard it over the radio—
like eye heard about miles' passing over the idiot tube—that you went home
surrounded by friends & peace, heard you wrote till you slipped into a coma
after you wrote a last poem called "fame and death,"
you left us great poems allen, poems that fused blues & jewish chants, rock 'n' roll
& jazz riffs you left behind as gifts to remind us of a life lived fast to the fullest,
in "absolute defiance," you were a bridge between the sacred,
the transcendental, the underground demon & the buddhist-shaman-priest,
you were the guru speaking of wars when skulls were used to cradle silver coins
flashing under the light of human skin stretched tight into lampshades
used to filter heat from glaring lightbulbs—& the silver flashing there
like glittering smiles, evil as death—o great bard breathing in & out,
spoken blues chants coursing through your lines gone home to rest,
gone home to rest beside your mother & father in spirit & shivah,
it was a great love you gave us, allen, a great love that makes me remember
you now with affection & awe, o great son of whitman, blake, & williams,
your love of mystery, gemara, your love of flesh & magic, blood of poetry
coursing through choruses of your river-veins, love
coursing through memory of chicken soup, roasted eggs, love,
the smell of challah bread evoking candles burning on the sabbath,
on the lower east side where you walked hip-di-dip, a little strut & bounce
in the dip of your stride, you walked amongst jews wearing yarmulkes—
& though you moved a little odd down there on passover,
buddhist that you were, you still moved,
many of them will still sit seven days of shivah for you,
many will lift their voices in solemn kaddish prayers—
& so eye baptize you here with rhythms of black church gospel,

with rhythms pulled from some of your favorite voices—
ray charles, bessie smith, ma rainey, charlie parker, & john coltrane—
have washed your memory down with holy cadences—cool & hot
as water—rinsed in blues & jazz riffs, chanted from voices
& baptized in holy rivers of cabala, cabala lore,

cabala, cabala lore, cabala, cabala lore

& blood & choruses, blood & choruses,
baptized in rivers of blood & choruses

cabala, cabala lore, cabala, cabala lore

coursing through poetry that burst from your river-veins,
coursing through poetry that burst from your river-veins,

shalom o great mystic bard, shalom

# WORDS THAT BUILD BRIDGES TOWARD A NEW TONGUE

you begin with a sound wrapped around a syllable, or syllables,
a word (or words) like razzmatazz, or ratamacue, then you listen to
a red-boned black man playing a horn like a clue,
like a train or john coltrane or bird, then you play around with sounds
your ears done heard, lift them off a rebound, spellbound inside a rue,
because of a cue your memory remembered & knew,
                                        now you add a few nouns & vowels,
words singing like birds, flying through a spring wind thunder clapping,
            with roiling, rolling consonants, their feathers echoing colors now
black or white or blue, as a ranky dank pressing flesh beneath them
was immune to trailing blues stretched out behind him,
voices that flew rhythmic as queued soundtracks through the night's
sweet longing, choo-chewing like wailing engines hurtling down isolated
                        tracks, way out in the dead of night's hushed music,
            around the voodoo, bewitching hour of bats, who like words
bruising from a crew of mad hatter good old boys were circling inside
a hushed cave, where a strange blend of language was fashioning itself now
from cries & screams, the whooshing of beating wings
drumming pell-mell clues through
            the dark cinematography of a dream bordering on nightmare,
as it wraps itself around you now as would a cocoon,

you find yourself there inside the cave of your head
& you are whatever it is you think you are there, brand new,
you are what you believe in as truth, right then, right there,
when you hear sheets of sound rushing out of the bell of a saxophone,
it is a stomp down cornucopia of magic spiraling out of a dream,
from a golden axe, shaped like an elephant's trunk, the shape of need here
is a question mark bewitching us with breath, power, mystery, stealth,
is what new language is shaping itself into now inside the neon air
hip-hopping & rapping in voice rhymes of young people,
before us right now is what the mind's ear reminds the tongue of here,
chasing the sound of a freight train moving at full speed, is a syntax,
a jackety-jack of wheels rolling through the slick flow of tracks bedazzling gears,

the song of it all beguiling us with amazement, the rackety-rack of steel spinning
over & down rails, underground or overground, tracks,

                                        the sound we hear is real when we know it
coming from the terrifying mystery of a hip shaman's horn,
we see the music form in the shape of the hot tongue of a bic flame lighter
tonguing out gushed heat,

                    flames as sounds, as words inside the scorched flow of lava,
inside a tongue that is red, white, & blue, laced with dues paid in philadelphia,
    in hamlet, north carolina, where a language was fractured there,
congealed, until it hopscotched itself to its own back beat
conundrum, before it pealed across the air clear as a bell ringing cold
on sundays, unleashed a rage in rhythm & tempo, heated voices in sermons,
became a fire there in flight, was volcanic with syllables aglow, the night
flaming with embers washing through the breeze like a tribe of fireflies
swarming the night sky, a voice pure & guttural,

                    a primal scream looping clues of prophecy here, blue,
or sweetly singing as a slew of birds

                        tracking across a fondued sky laced with magenta,
their music heard in ringing silver bells as the wind tongue trills melodic
as it breezes lilting language through chiming leaves trembling

like lovers in heat/time, when the air is all aglow & splendiferous
with greens, yellows, & golds,

                    bright reds of bougainvilleas,
jacarandas fragrant as voices of doves cooing, sweet pink of flaring
rhododendrons that burst into shapes of trumpet bells evoking
miles playing muted live in memory, clean as a whistle,
is where a poet stretches rubber sentences into bridges of music now,
language reinventing itself daily out of lost & found words,
constructing what it is to speak as a true american here,
today, right now, words moving through poems as magicians through parades,
clowns dressed up as verbs, adverbs, adjectives surrounding nouns with bright
verve, reminds the senses of sweet odor of frangipani perfume,
rhymes & rhythms intoxicating the senses,

this moment sluicing across the air in a rainbow of races,
seductive with music, images moving quickly as faces in an mtv video,

across screens blazing fast as beats moved through bebop, urban slick
as hip-hop brothas chilling wicked in blooming fubu color schemes
rad in baggy jeans, their hand jive flicking & stabbing the air, constantly blur-
                  ring images—blink & they're gone like pop goes the weasel—
their rhythms nicking edges off slick time in stop-gap measures,
voices locking & leaking into currency, flip & zip,
can-you-dig-it, inside blaring boxes clocking back beats stitching threads
through the culture of hip-hop, attitudes holding everything together there,
as when a guitar player picks blaze out of funk noise,
his cadence up inside & outside time,
as in this poem swinging its voice downwind to cross fragile bridges
strung together with cadences & words, structures underneath
form the bass-groove swaying back & forth over deep chasms,
between mountains of language, where a child hears vocabulary in a swing,
in the backyard of a favorite uncle waxing real with his sho-nuff-to-god,
hope-to-die-ace-boon-coon-throw-downs,
                        the ones that always got his back each & every
time he smacks scary, wherever he goes, their attitudes high-fivin their eyes
& everything silent here except the wind's screaming terror,
words trying to cross over to the other side, to where the nephew swings,
                  right here, right now, words flowing through seamless
as eye (w)rap my tongue around a bridge of johnny ace or nat king cole
stitching together a profusion of sweet cadences frank
sinatra & elvis stole, words that breathe inside a living language full of colors,
as choirs of birds singing atop hot telephone wires carry aretha's gospel,
a symphonic elocution of elegant voices,
               a cecil taylor bedazzlement of lyrical, discordant chords,
swinging double-bladed axes cutting down trees as they slice through all this
blue air, the bird man still singing now over steel tracks
snaking through & in between landscapes, where tupac & biggie now sleep
beside coaltrain(s) blowing through the night's voodoo air, sweet
the feeling here now, still blue as you were charlie parker,
& truly american as slow trains choo-chooing twelve bar blues
through your old stomping ground of kansas city's twelfth & vine,
where you first showed your razzle-dazzle,

　　　　　your feathers spreading their beauty through wind-chimes,
aching with your soliloquizing voice, always on edge,
triple-timing the fire that flowed through your genius ire on time,
until a chicken bone stuck itself inside your throat & damned up your music,
(like that legendary finger stuck in that dike did to tupac, did to biggie, too)
pure smack snaking venom through your veins,
in a deadly slow dance with death you stumbled & scratched,
poisoned your brain until your head nodded off for real, then the bells tolled,
but boy did you jam, jam, boy did you jam until you left, no sweat, boy did you
jam, jambo, jambalaya, gumbo, boy did you jam jam, boy did you jam
& play that horn for real before the pain jammed vomit in your throat,
left those hot cadences cold as methuselah,
fire bird of stricken-heat, chicken-gumbo boy of sound language, boy,
did you jam, jam, boy did you jam, boy did you jam, jam, boy did you jam
riffs run through scales & chords, inverting electric

everything you heard you turned inside out, structures,
blew past every note—& through them, too—
rooted them in your own blue expression of turn everything inside out,
you jambo, gumbo, chicken-liver boy, running up & down jambalaya scales,
pastiche, a coaltrain before coltrane blew down the hushed voodoo night,
a coaltrain burning across flat plains of kansas city, flight & barbecue
sauce up in the flavor of your drenched hot giddiup, scorching as red pepper
chili sauce, yo boy of bebop phrasing in *groovin' high,* you blew:

*bebop, bebop, beedoo beeboli, doodle-li, bebop, bebop,*
*beedoo beeboli, doodle-li, bebop, bebop,*
*beedoo beeboli*

　　　　　　　　　　　　*bop baw baw baw bo de baaaaaaaaa daaaaaaa* . . . . . . . .

& you ran it all the way to new york city, minton's & birdland,
chicken eating boy turned hip man skeedaddleing choochooing chords,
so fast the air could hardly digest them, not to mention some human
ears, playing *salt peanuts, salt peanuts,*
you & diz beautiful beyond words tradin' fours in duet,
fours in traffic, boppin & rappin before tupac & biggie were even born

bird, you uptown in harlem creating language that reinvented itself again
& again before rap seduced rhythms down to scratching old records & words,
skating over samples of james brown & george clinton, toasting & roasting
the language like you & diz did in a *dizzy atmosphere,* jammin'

*beedle-loo-beedle-loo-beedle-loo-bop,*
*beedle-loo-beedle-loo-beedle-loo-bop,*
*beedle-loo, beedle-loo-beedle-loo-bop,*
*beedle-loo, beedle-loo*
*beedle-loo-beedle-loo-beedle-loo-bop,*
*beedle-loo-beedle-loo-beedle-loo-bop,*
*beedle-loo-beedle-loo-beedle-loo-bop,*
*beedle-loo, beedle-loo*

words & sounds building bridges toward a new tongue,
& it all started back in africa, mixed with europe over here, everything else,
found itself here, too, in this gumbo stew, jambalaya,
this salad bowl filled with all kinds of flavors,
this pastiche, collage of language reinventing itself every day,
every moment giving itself props, wherever words are
spoken, patch themselves together with sound, form a sentence,
that becomes a musical line perhaps lifted from armstrong, bird, or miles
a phrase snatched & grafted into language of tupac & biggie, buzzing
in the attitudes of alanis morrisette or jamiroquai scatting
phrases metamorphosed into dance when he reaches back
to grab hold of a language to swing & sing

today, in this moment in time, when everything is evolving,
right now, from cue tips of tongues, a new language
is waiting for you to discover listener, for you to give it some props,
to speak it, wrap your tongue around it, roll it off your assembly line of new
expressions too, so give it up for the new, right here, right now, so speak it,
don't diss it, give the new some props right now,
freak it out with your own
dash of flavor,
                        say what's up in the air as sound, now
know it's rooted & shaped in the vortex of truth-change,
constant with language & words, sounds & attitude now,

say what's birthing in the womb of air, now
say what's birthing in the womb of air, now:

*bustin on the scene clockin banji beastie boys actin like fiends:*
*down with the fave, funky jam, the noise up in the legit*
*jack up, someone screaming to kill the ill funky noise living large,*
*with an ace keepin it real, poppin the rip, doin the nasty to the bump*
*breakdown in the bricks, where the homies roll bones*
*to clock dollars, chillin hard through the calendar, gangstas flexin*
*profiles, while they kick it on the real decked in doo-doo pants*
*saggin slow like low riders over their doggy-grips*
*as they watch aces ball with the pill takin it hard to the rack,*
*skyin down the box, risin up like god to deal, or flash for the count,*
*pumpin treys from downtown, nothin but nets*

words that build bridges toward a new tongue

*beedle-loo-grab-a-groove-drop-some-slick-talk,*
*jazz-a-phrase-pop-a-blues-new-as-hip-hop,*
*cruisin-through-rapping-clues-sprung-from-bebop*
*me-&-you, grooving through*
*me-&-you, groovin through*

*me-&-you, singin new . . . . .*

# 8

---

NEW POEMS, 2000–2001

# IN REMEMBRANCE OF YOU, ITALO

*for Italo Scanga, painter & sculptor (1932–2001)*

I.

you were a beautiful spirit italo, strong, enabling, father to five,
grandfather to the same number, companion to su-mei-yu,
you always gave more than we ever could imagine, a consummate artist,
you, with one foot anchored in the old world peasant stock of saints
& fables, mountains & deeply severe country people dressed in black,
suspicious madonnas & a glinting cross hanging like a wicked blade,
or a lynched man around the neck & against the dark backdrop
of a tunic-robe, worn by a humble priest in your village of lago
cosenza-calabria, italy, where bony dogs & fear of fear itself were rooted
in the soil where you were born & the new one here of flash & laid back,
but cutting-edge, show & tell new money by the pacific,
new age scientists & engineers, who wave checkbooks with no limits
sitting under fragrant eucalyptus trees, on the campus of ucsd,
in la jolla, california, america, where you began to tangle up everything
inside rich profusions—christ & pythagoras, trombones & tree
trunks, seashells & garish figurines, trinkets you attached to free-
standing assemblages & meta this & meta that, meta, meta, meta-
laughter & joy in what you did inside transmogrified
within the kiln of your creative imagination, a thing to behold,
it expressed itself in a celebration of strong, primary colors,
deep, luminous blues, canary yellows, sunset red-oranges, incredible globes,
blood red & stunning as those splotched & grown all over the earth,

eye knew you were a master when eye first met you eleven quick years ago,
when eye moved to la jolla, from the big apple,
saw it in the power in which your language expressed itself—
a visual poetry for all to see, stroked & fashioned in bold metaphors—
you sought out & found at flea markets, swap meets, which you scavenged
on weekend mornings like an archaeologist excavating for sacred objects—
which you were—you looked for saws, washboards, old beat-up violins,
tubas, anything thrown away: an old school globe
transformed in your hands into a head, or the belly of a stick-

figure striding through a world where animals are endangered
as is great music, poetry, or art: a gaunt dog on patrol, looking for food
inside the hallucinogenic nature of our world, our fears,
all things imagined, or real, served as grist for the mill
in your magical, sleight-of-hand tricks—now
you see it, now it's not what you thought you saw
for us to move through, made over by your shamanistic,
transforming élan—visions of both old & new worlds—

you had already taken a bite out of new york city
at your solo whitney show, in 1972,
& though it was a big deal for you when margaret
opened an art gallery & asked you for a show,
you said, "why not" & did it,
though you had already won me over with your smile
larger & brighter than any daybreak—
it was that gesture that spoke volumes
about you, what you believed in,
what you were put on earth for—to make art

& you did with a fury, turned every simple object
you touched into the way you saw the world,
through cubism & folk influences, meta this, meta that, meta, meta, meta,
a mode of expression, a kind of transformative rhythm you struck
in the way a figure stood, the angle of sculptural language that evoked
myth & legend collaged into pictures, standing next to cypress trees,
their slender branches & leaves flaring like a butane lighter
flame shooting skyward, next to a skull,
old world drinking jugs made of clay, pottery, & ceramics,
& an old house hovering above chickens glazed in glass, a shoe,
a surreal face & a violin so we wouldn't forget music,
you made paintings within paintings, squared off other worlds
bursting with a profusion of colorful dots that exploded
into the viewer's vision like the big bang
shooting meteors like a swarm of shotgun pellets,

your studio was a place in & of itself, unique, unbelievable,
what you crammed into what used to be an old auto shop—
endless cages filled with mad, singing birds, taxidermy, old religious relics,
all manner of tools & discarded objects you had picked up, stored for later
use in your art, which you sometimes hated to sell,
so it was crammed there, too, along with books & your music,
which you listened to every morning—operas, arias, sonatas
& that fragrant smell of fruit trees outside, in your yard,
& all those jars of different olives in your kitchen,
& you there stirring the pots like a mad scientist

you were the real deal—walking upright on earth, italo,
who didn't check your feelings at whatever door you walked through
& now we all have to deal with the horrible news—that you won't be
walking through our doors again
though your spirit will always remain with us


   2.

on that day you were in the kitchen cooking italian
sausage & beans, making homemade pasta,
you were dancing & singing, italo,
caught up in creating another one
of your celebrated meals everyone drooled for,
beautiful & life-giving you were inside your spirit that was far
too large for that short, compact body of yours that worked
every day so very hard to hold it all in check
(like that cone-shaped body of dirt & rock
had always tried, but failed, to hold in check
that volatile spirit beneath mt. etna)

& even as you were singing & dancing & celebrating
your spirit was beginning to leave us—when did you know,
dear italo, when did you feel the moment upon you?
you keeled over with joy still flowing trough your spirit
& your oversized heart gave way, left you like the ancestors
you always painted & brought us all to tears—
it was a sudden thing, italo, the best way to go—

& now you have been transmogrified into ash, my friend—
like the spirit climbing free from inside mt. etna—
to keep & rest in an urn created especially for you

we will miss you my dear friend,
we will miss you, but will hold close your memory in our hearts,
O lover of poetry, music, & great food, joy & laughter,
we will miss you son of lago, cosenza-calabria, italy,
we will hold close your memory in our hearts
as long as ours keep beating,

we will hold close your memory in our hearts, breathing

BULLETIN FROM THE IDIOT TUBE

one day while eating a fish sandwich, waiting for a connection,
eye heard a bulletin breaking through miami's airport
idiot-tube-tv (which was filled with all kinds of accents stirred inside
languages mixed up like jambalaya, or one-pot stews)
that someone crafty had invented a snap-on holder for a ratty toupee
in new york city (where appearances count for everything these days,
whether you're raggedy-butt, black-tied, or a funky asshole,
because all of it counts in the good old big apple),
where all a balding man has to do is snap
                                                his hairpiece in place
(four snaps popped into holders with glue on top of a shining bald pate,
smooth as an unbroken egg, will do it)
& voila, no more fretting over flapping toupees sailing away
                                        like flying squirrels through windstorms,
unless, that is, one or two snaps are left undone,
then a tongue of breeze might be able to get up under that
slicked down vanity rug,
cause it to start billowing like a tent rising & falling,
straining hard at its limits as the other snaps try to hold it down,
its language all of a sudden ever-more lopsided now, in a panic
even, as gravity pulls it everwhichaway, in this scenario
the wind's breath might probe through any opening it finds,
        stick its tongue right through to pry & break the snaps' grip.

this brings to mind what seems to happen all the time
down in the nation's capital, when you watch blow-hard,
rug-wearing congressmen going back & forth, on one thing or another,
their egos rising & falling like wind-blown tents,
hairpieces billowing, unsnapping, straining at their limits

RANDOM MISHAPS

it is summer on the streets of anywhere in the world,
where bee-hived cities are swarming with people,
eye am here in the middle of a conveyor-belted sidewalk
& a man with a penis hanging out of his nose hops by
scowling, he balances himself on a cane,
because one foot the size of a rat's claw is suspended,
and the other spread out wide & flat as a rug
in the shape of a goose's size twenty, huge as a clodhopper
& one eye looks at you hard as an indigo-blue marble,
the other, warm as a brown piece of bread
lying burnt on a scorched sand dune,
darts here & there like scattering roaches after
a light is turned on in the dead space after midnight

& as we speak through the nodding of heads
(his a peanut on top of a humpty-dumpty sack of woe body,
mine a dreadlocked watermelon atop a big pear)
he licked out a lizard tongue quickly, caught a fly for lunch,
then rolled it back fast into his mouth like a venus flytrap
(or a bear market eating up money faster than some people think
of suicide when numbers flicker down the big stock market board
in a blink, becoming a free fall, then the free fall
becomes a howling avalanche),
then you notice the scaled finger pointing right at you
(or somewhere the eyeball is hightailing it to)
& it reminds you of a darting coral snake about to strike,
right before you notice his elbow yawning open
a tiny mouth full of little sharp monkey teeth
& this makes you think of those piranha fish that darted
like killer bees here & there, that time you didn't go

swimming in that murky river in brazil that was
muddier then the incredibly shrinking mississippi,
now full of two-headed, one-legged frogs hopping around,

like some clueless congressmen,
then you see it when he lifts his size twenty
goose-foot, see it rolling around down there, getting a fix,
taking dead aim at you, and it seems watery,
reminds you of the one eye set dead center
in the forehead of goliath

with a rock thrown from david's trusty slingshot,
now you see it clearly when he lifts a flopping foot to take a step,
& you see it is a green eye looking hard at you as his other marble
& it's rolling around down there under a big, long toe that is
hanging free from the loose straps of a leather sandal
& you wonder why it doesn't squash every time
he drops his foot down like a rock, then a light goes on inside
your head (just as his rat's claw curls into a ball up in the air,
suspended above asphalt) like a warning:
                              maybe these are random

mishaps, errors of genetic cloning & just maybe,

perhaps, you are looking at the future
& don't understand that it's all really real,

don't understand where it all went wrong

# FLYING PREDATORS

butcherbird-shrikes, jackiehangmen, murderbirds
impale victims onto needle-sharp thorns, string them out
like ornamental trophies, hang them grotesque
from weird christmas trees the males use to display rotting kills,
to catch lovers with their savvy skill to murder, hang some as warnings
to protect territory—the great, gray shrike, a small, flying killer
whale, feeding on sparrows, kangaroo rats, lizards,
reminds me of the way some crazed white people have attacked
the entire world, today, they are blurring fastballs zooming
down from wires, snatching up their prey in hooked beaks,
armed with teeth, called shrikes because of their shrieking, high-
calling sound of death, catching, eating anything their size allows—
they hang the corpses from spikes of yucca trees, in a strange
ritualized, celebration of death, that reminds—in many ways—
of the madness of humans devouring the world, today

# 9/11 EMERGENCY CALLS COMING INTO MANHATTAN

### 1.

a crystal clear morning greeted you, dazzlingly blue
as a sweet water lagoon on some caribbean island
is blue, blue as the beautiful eyes of some
swedish woman is blue, as the deep true licks on the guitar
voice of robert johnson is blue, the alto riffings of charlie yard-
bird parker is blue, blue as a blue dress
lady day's voice wore, searching for meaning in "strange fruit,"
blue as miles davis on "blue in green" is blue, coltrane on "alabama,"
blue as the sky death flew & turned into a flying missile,
a flying coffin, a heartless bomb glinting silver after sun rays
struck it, glanced off as it flew low in the blue sky just above roof tops
& chimneys, flying true as an arrow aimed true
at the heart of new york city, this first glinting missile coming
straight in from the north is blue, as it struck the world trade center
north tower, high up, is blue, blue as a fireball igniting tonguing
flames turning to smoke billowing upward, outward, blue as screams
wailing & piercing through the darkness, flames eating through steel,
flashing teeth of heat chewing, blue as horror of people
stunned for the first time to panic, into real fear after leaving loved ones
at home & somehow & somewhere behind them the terrible slow
feeling begins creeping through the bones, seizes the heart
with the terrible possibility that this could be it,
*but it couldn't be,* because some of you have just arrived
& it's morning & it's dazzlingly clear & blue, a brighter blue even
than the policemen in uniform downstairs who just greeted you
blue & beautiful & warm as caribbean waters are crystal blue
this time of year, when you look out into blue space
you see the second coffin of death arriving out of the south,
it strikes the heart of the twin spirit of the skyline, you watch it erupt,
become a twin fireball, then you know, all who have seen it now know
what terror is, really feels like, is the dread you are thinking of now,
what is running like madness through your heart & brain,
horror is what you feel suddenly now in all of this,
your life flashing before you now as if it were a movie,

as some seeing it live & on tv thought is was a movie, but not you,
so you move with the others toward the windows high up in the blue—
some move like sleepwalkers, others screaming hysterically loud—
move toward the clear windows you loved so totally to look out of
as the flames, smoke, heat & terror increase—
*tell me it is a movie,* you thought, *a hollywood thriller*
*& arnold, or bruce will come rescue us all soon, very soon—*
& you thought you could see your god from up here,
inside, behind all this clear glass, where you took in such expanses,
such power you felt, so high up, each & every day coming here,
to witness all this sweeping glory was a miracle, now this sudden fear,
this swelling madness burning a black hole through the miracle that is
now a place of overwhelming fear, crawling like bile to grip
your spirit in your stomach, as the billowing smoke blooms
& flames keep licking toward you as you move with co-workers,
move toward the blown-out windows, what were you thinking
as you climbed out on that ledge, a fierce wind up here licking,
whipping around you like an avenging spirit, taking your breath
away as you looked down, then stepped out into nothingness,
tumbled head over heels, your clothes flapping & tearing
wildly around you, the wind screaming, like you, for a moment,
then it was over before it was over, though you knew what
you saw before the end as truth, what were you thinking
out there, when you saw the whole building imploding down,
coming toward you like the hairy brown-gray legs of a tarantula
spider, crawling down the sides of your beloved second home,
so ominous now as it pancaked down, floor-by-floor at you,
toward chief ganci, father judd giving final rites & so many others
& when you hit rock bottom it all fell hard on top of you roaring,
choking acid smoke billowing as from a phylogenic cloud
after a volcanic eruption incinerated the day,
then everything went black, black as the skins of delta blues
singers from mississippi, whose voices imploded before they rose,
rose back up like tonguing flame & smoke billowing black there,
before they wrapped their black voices blue-black around song
& turned pitch-black nights, tar-baby nights into blue days,
down in the scorched earth grounds of unknown lynched bones,
those black voices full of blue tones of raise-up redemption . . .

but there, at ground zero, when the hush fell down,
the voices went silent as ghost-people emerged
& things would never, ever be the same again,
things would never, ever be the same . . .


    2.
9/11 emergency calls coming right at you
9/11, emergency calls screaming

what were they thinking as they steered flying bombs,
flew them straight into their targets,
what were they thinking. "why did they hate us so?"
freaked out voices mutter

9/11 emergency call coming right at you

did we look into their eyes, how deep back inside themselves
they were, burrowed back in their skulls, cold as pinpoints,
because they had left all feelings behind,
inside experiences they had gone through full of chanting prayers
five times a day, that brought them to this moment of redemption,
high up in the crystalline blue, confused people all around them,
going through fear, rage, quiet acceptance
until they saw the towering symbols of capitalism before them—
those seemingly impregnable double edifices of everything
wall street stood for; power, arrogance, hubris & money—
standing before them now, so very clear, so hard-on phallic,
looming & glittering like millions of razors when sunrays hit them,
glancing off those 43,000 windows, they were coming closer to now
they were so very clear, looming, coming closer until
everyone who didn't know suddenly knew,
as the flying bombs held on course straight as a crow flies,
or a screaming arrow from the bow of an expert,
everyone knew now as they flew into the looming hard-ons,
erect with the blood of gold, silver & greenbacks & hubris,
they knew as their panic shattered into countless shards of fear,
as those 43,000 windows that were razors glinting
when sunrays hit them suddenly blew out now

like the pinpoint eyes of those who flew the bombs
blew out at the moment of impact, prayers chanting in their heads,
then we suddenly knew, right before the world suddenly knew,

heard 9/11 emergency calls coming straight through
9/11, 911
                        emergency calls
coming straight at you


    3.

it was a castration, pure & simple, a cutting off of phallic symbols
of greed, money & hubris, they came down blooming clouds,
blowback coming to wall street, turning it into a war zone,
a war zone of weeping, screaming, unreal horror,
clouds black as those delta blues singers, color gloomed now
this once blue day, gone now, like the gold coin we knew this morning
as the sun was gone now, like those once gleaming phallic edifices,
everything down here was shrouded in mourning dustcoats,
as if in a movie, stunned ghost people stumbled through streets
ankle deep in soot & paper, wrecked fire wagons, police cars
& bodies—what was left of them—& street lights glittering through
the unreal light like flashing hyena teeth,
blink down on paper clips, chairs, telephones, pieces of bone,
shoes, blood & guts, shocked eyeballs looking up mute from the soot,
glinting earrings next to hats, an arm, office supplies, pieces of paper
fluttering through the stinging air like bat wings,
gone now the innocence, gone the hubris of impregnability,
gone now the arrogance, the jaunty hautiness in the step,
in its place this new blueness, a blueness of spirit, of whatever
the future holds, a blueness of not knowing what you thought
you knew, who the person standing next to you was, is, is he an arab,
is he,—or she—a terrorist, what does an arab look like anyway
without a head wrap, or veil? a jew, an italian, an american indian,
who, what? who? what? who? what? who? do they look like
mirrors of ourselves? ghost people hiding in corners?
white people full of anger? who hate everythingabouttoday,
like timothy mcveigh whoblewupthenotionwhitepeoplecouldn'tbe
terrorists&noonepointedfingersat them, even after

the uni-bombertheodorekocinskiblewup those people
with those booby-trap letter-bombs, so who is a stranger,
who can know you now, since you don't know who you are yourself,
you don't even know what you're thinking even now as you speak,
because it changes from day to day, from whatever is said on tv,
talking heads on talk radio shows, all the flag waving now,
all this saber-rattling jingoism, boiling talk of war,
it is a blueness of revenge burning
red-hot through the language of the day—
though this, too, in time will calm down, fade away—
shown daily now—though this, too, will fade in time—on tv screens,
it reminds you of surreal disaster movies made in hollyweird,
swarming with high-beamed lights, thousands of made-up
extras, who shuffle through their shots with bone-weary faces,
like ghost people, as shadows of soldiers with machine guns
drift through the horror that is palpable now—
though this, too, will wind up & fade away—imprints
in soot the form of a footprint, a hand clawing as if for clean air,
an upturned face frozen into a wooden mask at ground zero,
though it looks like a movie this is real
terror & panic, frazzled voices, real, the stumbling strides of ghosts,
the plumes of gray-black-brown smoke belching, flaring upwards
to blanket this eerie, sacred burial ground of pulverized dust/rubble,
soot-coats worn by heroic firemen & rescue people,
all races of weary volunteers from everywhere,
this spot marked forever by a jagged six-story tombstone—
                              which, too, in time will be taken away—

all that is left of two gleaming 110 story towers,
two phallic symbols seared into memory & onto postcards

& 9/11, an emergency call sweeping through manhattan,
engulfing the pentagon, exploding in pennsylvania,
spreading out to ensnare most of the globe
9/11, emergency calls wailing through all of this . . .

& what is terrorism but a faceless, invisible presence
suddenly here, there, completely in your midst,

then gone, then back again,
like a sudden death on a highway in the form of someone
drunk & out of control, in a runaway car hurtling right at you,
perhaps, a mind-set blowing your world apart on a bright, clear day
in september, or anytime, like now,
in this eerie time of the world

where there are two gaping holes
in the snaggle-tooth skyline of downtown manhattan,
two gaping, empty holes that ask questions,
are silently screaming for forgiveness & redemption,
two gaping holes that beg the questions

will we ever be able to fake inncence again,
howdy doody cornball smiles, daffy duck head-in-the-ground,
black-birds-sitting-on-a-wire-in-a-row-follow-the-leader,
wherever the bushies say go, "let's roll,"
in this land of redwhite&blueapplepieflagwavingbombers?

doesn't all this saluting remind anyone of the slippery slope
germans found themselves on heil hitlering genocide back in the day?

will citizens become suspect for not waving the flag,

will things will ever be about peace & sanity & love & respect
& different opinions listened to anywhere in america, now,
anywhere in the western, christian world?

9/11 emergency calls coming straight through to you,

9/11 wake-up calls, wake-up calls, wake-up calls

ringing up in the air, coming straight to you,

sluicing through the soiled air voices of the blues

coming straight at you, straight at you . . .

# MOVING TOWARD THE OPEN, THE LIGHT

1.

you begin underneath all that concrete,
down inside corridors, labyrinthine
tubes that fan out like secret passageways,
come together in a place called the pipe gallery,
where signs point to danger, no smoking signs
beneath raw sludge sedimentation tanks,
where arrows pointing east & west, north & south
move us through corridors, up toward the light,
toward the exit sign, up a beveled, flat ramp,
stretching like a concrete tongue toward the yellow
light, just above the entranceway, over transparent,
soiled, dangling strips of plastic that flap—
like madmen waving their tongues & arms in a frenzy,
when they are hungry for something, anything—chard even—
their frazzled minds tell them they desire—
when the ocean wind stirs up, speaking in tongues,
drum rhythms in waves into rock & sand, craggy shores,
tonguing in from the west to tickle the sashaying, dirty
strips that waver, ripple, & move like dancers
as they form a kind of doorway you must go through,
from here to there, to reach the low, concrete wall,
so you can look out to where the water meets sky,
& where you are climbing toward now,
so you can see the muted, sometimes dazzling light,
always suffused with veils of pelting mist that prick
your face looking out as the pacific roars in
quick, speaking in tongues, cascading rhythms

2.

& on a clear day when you move up & out from here,
up this concrete tongue that is a ramp, that leads to the top—
you move past two gray walls, that form a kind of chute,
you move up toward the low, concrete wall,

beyond which first you hear, then you see the miracle
laid out before you—the pacific seems so calm, placid even
when you cast out your eyes like a fisherman would his line
& hooks whatever dream fish he is looking for—
but when you look directly down you see the boiling edges
of rage foaming & spitting when the waves show their disappointment,
the journey has been spent, now you are beyond the concrete chute,
even the man sweeping dirt up the hill, up the concrete tongue,
beyond the secret passageways, the labyrinthine tubes,
the pipe gallery full of signs poining in all directions,
now you are here, free of all you left behind, out in the open air,
you are crossing the street, where before, in this poem,
it was all about your imagination, what you thought
you would see & hear & now you are here, crossing the street—
like a deer crossing wide-eyed an empty road,
out in the middle of nowhere, looking for those dreaded twin lights
hurtling toward it, like its mother or father spoke of so many times
before—& you have come to the precipice to view
the pacific's mystery & power, stretching out before you now,
palm trees on your left & right, seals below, frolicking
on large wet rocks, in front of coves,
then you see the splendid power of it all, beyond what
you imagined it would be, out beyond the face of this wall,
the waves rolling in, speaking in tongues continuously,
continuous as your abiding faith has been always ambushed,

flabbergasted by the repetition of miracles here, always,

like there, right now, in front of your eyes, right now

## RECONFIGURATIONS

there are moments when we are what we think we are,
bright suns burning deep with love, white moons glowing,
lighting up the sweltering darkness, beauty,
the center of our imagination,
but when revisiting old music, rhythms are sometimes heard
in a fresh light, a language you thought you knew
now sounds radically different
in the way a musical phrase suddenly turns,
makes your body move in a way you had hadn't known possible
before, shows you, once again, surprise is always lurking
within a moment of deep creation,

so you follow this new way of hearing,
a kind of reinvention in your ears, so to speak,
it reminds you of a time you once knew, heard, without notice,
a flaring cadence butaning a fragrant night sky
inside a voice, a piece of music rooted in an expression suddenly
there, transforming itself, is both familiar & unfamiliar, but there
anyway, new, your faculties refitted, retooled
fresh inside the center of your imagination,
where you had refitted your faculties, retooled them
without knowing—the way you took things in—
perhaps you had fallen in love,
or dropped out of love, who can say—
but it had happened anyway, was some kind of miracle
the way you had reconfigured things
inside your spirit—red things turned into blue,
metaphors pinwheeled into stars, became
a kind of fireworks of language holding brilliant
words, chords, shining faces spangling the darkness

where you lived, caterpillars became butterflies,
babies killers, geometry architecture,
night day, noise music, sounds ordered & shaped into forms,

poetry sprang alive transformed by new images inside language,
the way the voice digs itself out of a dark hole & breathes
again in light, fresh air, is a miracle, eye tell you now,
again & again, that reconfiguration is a miracle

& a miracle is always a blessing

# FRAGMENTED SOLOS, PATTERNS & TEXTURES;
# OTHER WORLDS; THE PAINTINGS OF PHILIP TAAFE

images float against backgrounds, fossils, shells
splotched blue, green, deep-sea fish
are speckled, a dream edged with white, iridescent
diatoms, amoebas, multiple worlds membraned & pulsing
clouds scarabesque, they glow three-times-four equal squared,
twelve worlds in total, they bob up crustaceans, seaweeds
in some transparent world of water hold shape,
then burst like cool fireworks deep in a night sky
on fourth of july, are prayers, meditations,

                          all star-like explosions
blooming red, pink, & yellow, blue,

as fire-engine scarlet spiders crawl over,
a desert floor blooms,
as stripe-hooded cobra snakes swarm bleached-out blues,
fern leaves curve like elk horns,
unsheathed daggers hook in pteris viscosa,
crabs that exchange clues float black & green
pincers against red, appear wicked as saber blades,
or supple as arms bent in motion of floating swimmers seen
from below as they stroke, touch fingers, tip to tip,
form oblong mouths that open to kiss,

here we see feelings patterned dense with ripples,
sluiced through deep canyons, terrains, sigiri strands,
textures, vipera russelli, breed swarming
shapes that twist & curve like bodies of snakes
green & black & blue, give rise to

a kind of visual, tribal language,
                          archaic & new, aural,

visual music the glue holding everything together within
rhythm, as in a kaleidoscope of movements
improvised & associative, colors—orange, green, yellow swirls—
squared in basic threes & fours, tempos & pacing, time
& cadence, mathematics & galaxies, distillations,
blooming star-bursts,
a four-cornered cutting thing that could be a weapon
carved out of a black backdrop,
could be a doorway the mind walks through to discover
an arabic world of patterns & textures, designs,
could be a space-dream cut-out high up in the night sky, a looming
wedge, a stencil,
        could be starfish & amoebas clustered behind a slit,
inside a transparent, caribbean-green body of water,
suddenly inked totally black,
could be whatever the imagination holds
when confronted by a sudden, improvised solo

& then swirls of calligraphy, white volta
& ferns—green & brown & maroon—wavering
tall, floating like dreamscapes,
                                a calligraphy of snakes,
prints composed & washing through perceptions like music
speckled against a beige, strata colensoi, graphics etched
hold an abstract notion of some inner city rhythms
cold-blooded as bands of black, white, & gray,
yellow lines oscillating patterns of connective,
crisscrossing conversations that suddenly break off,
become fragmented speech fused by gyrating waves of sound-
tracks, break dancing, seemingly random,
but held together inside a delicious mystery
of compelling music, linguistic tissue,

a kind of visual, tribal language,
archaic & new, aural,

where  art evokes an interplay between poetry & meaning,
where inner-spaces explode with words & worlds
translated into colors, which means anything the viewer sees
in them, their meaning held inside rooted imaginations,
where they can become other worlds, or sacred
objects pulsating strangeness & beauty—

fragmented solos of confusion & order—where danger
evokes a way of seeing, a conversation overheard

a kind of transcendent ritual
engagement that is magical—

creation in opposition to what is seen

## PULSE & BREATHE;
*for Charlie "Yardbird" Parker*


eye remember bone under skin as gristle of wings
beneath bird's feathered flights, solos, up in the tone,
music inside syllables echoing light, up in the steep night,
transparent as an ethereal shimmering,
as a shower of colors laced through the sight, is a necklace
of white pearls strung around a black woman's neck,
from where we stand with plumes of flares in our hands
we see her at the edge of a looming vortex,
as a fanfare of trumpets blooms from somewhere,
she starts to dance a fandango with herself
& everyone standing there, looking, is amazed

# WHAT THE POETIC LINE HOLDS

the line can be taut as a straight clothesline
strung across a patch of field full of sun-
flowers, a whip in the hand of a lion-tamer,
cracking out commands, a geometric groove between
two points, straight as an arrow flies true to the target,
like a flat jump shot leaving the hands of michael
jordan, with the game on the line, a ruled line,
upon which sets a string of words perched
like a flock of blackbirds gossiping high
up on a telephone wire, their dark shapes silhouettes
against a day sky, their black shapes holding true
forms a series of black hole seductions for our speech
to flow through, is like what improvisation does whenever
it changes up whatever is said inside & through a line like jazz
riffs, is perhaps what bird passed on to miles in an instant
of rare beauty, is what his sense of liberation was at that time
& so on & so forth, ad infinitum, on the other hand
the line can be as loose as a goose frolicking in clear water,
shaking a tailfeather baby, whatever the mind holds
true as its artistic inclination, is what the poetic line stretches
our deep limits out into, is a moment we can dive through,
find the other side & that is what possibly shapes the line,
whatever the imagination is able to manage,
hold onto, the music there following a snaking flow
of words, that act like notes embedded inside
a composition, is what the poetic line holds, clues,
perhaps a fragment, a sliver of bright sound,
glinting, as a gold tooth hit by a glancing ray of sun
can evoke a solo & so on & so forth, ad infinitum

## ONE SUMMER VIEW; IN PORT TOWNSEND, WASHINGTON

*for Sam Hamill*


soft blue wind caresses ease in off the sound,
the water's cool surface shimmers
blue diamond-rare, miles up in the air a trumpet slips
glittering hard licks true & fast, slick as a moment
eclipsed in a wink
                    & quick as a hairpin turn
you're looking out across the diamond-blue shimmering to see
a low, long land mass rising & swimming out to sea,
where the blue becomes a darker, deeper blue,

where the land's end is the brown-green
sandy snout of whidbey island, seemingly swimming—
a whale's head jutting—out to sea, then back over here again, where
green leaves brimming from branches & bushes are hands
waving *good-bye, good-bye,*
like farewells of weeping lovers,

now you see trees standing guard, high on black bluffs
overlooking the water, foaming death as it exhausts itself
washing ashore, as the trees above wave their branch-arms
everwhichaway, like a music conductor,
whenever the wind blows hard, the music
a serenade of flutes imitating the tongues of breezes,
this is what you see looking out the window of alexander's castle,
overlooking the straits of juan de fuca,
at the tip-end of port townsend, washington

everything serene here, blue, green, & brown, sun-
light dappling around edges, hard black masses—
the shape of shadows—spreading, over which one piercing birdcall
tingles, pricks the senses
as it wheels, slices its double-winged comma shape right through
the blue singing, like a solo of miles davis cutting right through,
clean to the heart, true as a surgeon's scalpel,

these moments are a shopping list of natural wonders,
beauty, all the things we ever imagined leaping off postcards
we receive from faraway locations,
most times always somewhere over *there,*
        on the flip side of imagination

& then bam! it's right there, dead center in a blind/spot,
clued into a glance, at the edge of where your eyes are looking,
just now, where your vision fell just short

& the moment completely escaped you

SPRING DAY IN LA JOLLA; 2000

seagulls wheel, dive, & slice their hooked wing tips,
clean as knife blades cutting through the blue,
up there they look like cut-out silhouettes,
reminscent of commas punctuating the wind's lisp,
while underneath the pacific hisses its speech of coiled rattlesnakes
its waves suddenly losing their fury, becoming spray
frothing after contacting sand & rock

all around, palm trees stand straight as sentries
manning posts outside english castles, here, in a row they shoot
skyward all around a beach & tennis club in la jolla,
bunched leaves & ferns atop their skulls wave like plumes
sprouting from helmets of swiss guards
standing guard at the vatican,

sometimes when the eye locates these images,
these similes, it is a matter of perception pricking
the imagination, is about how senses enter & co-inhabit
the image observed, like how a flight of sleek birds in a line, perhaps,
reminds of a beautiful sentence in a poem—
how they stitch themselves together overhead,
their dark bodies black as typed words strung out across a page,
the angles of their bodies like accents of speech,
lyrical as language sung by derek walcott,
the image as a line of black dots thrown upon a canvas,
or bullet holes that tattoo a lifeless body naked on bloody ground

& all things carry weight—equal or unequal—inside the imagination

& now, all of a sudden (surprise from out of the blue)
an epileptic fit of mist coughs in from the pacific
                    paralyzing the day for                    a moment,
is like a nightmare that enters a beautiful dream

before clearing

& my eyes once again lick a rug of bright tulips, red as a dazzling dress—
as my eyes sometimes devour the essence of beautiful women walking by—
hungry for the sun that now breaks through the billowing gray soup,
& is as welcome as a heartfelt love letter from a faraway place—

this warm sun bringing bright relief for everyone
gathered here on this, or any other gray, soup day

# FAST LANE
### for Victor Hernández Cruz

fast lane, the ball is up in the lights
& you are breathing hard, there
& wherever the flight of the sphere takes your eyes
in its arc, you find yourself there, chasing
the music of the curve, up in the air, slick as an eagle,
or a red-tailed hawk, when it turns & dives,
its wing tip become a blade,
sharp as its beak breaking the flesh of prey

& from here you are there, too,
inside the blood-letting, the death of the prey
horrible, but pulsating as an image
inside your imagination
& you are riding a wave of creation inside your mind,
a current of light & air that takes you to a fertile place
inside that imagination, deep down within, perhaps,
an imaginary circle, where you now consider
the path of the ball as it flies arching
through the blue, it is a cut-out object,
an image, black as a period on a white page,
then you fast-break your mental juices forward,
your improvising twists & turns inside
the possibility that you can do whatever
this thing you thought you could do,

& it, like you, is running backward,
way up inside the music
you are listening to, now, inside your head,
you move the tempo forward, because it is your own
creation, way forward, past the dot up in the blue,
that is black now as any moment you considered
murder as an answer, then shrugged it off,
as one would a coat swarming with fleas & flies,
then you bevel yourself into a groove,

but very much still on time,
inside this moment you are creating for yourself
now, you are present there, but here, too,
on this page, looking out at yourself,
but that can get very boring,

so you press pedal to the metal & shoot
your mind out ahead, running fast
as the image of that brown bird with spinning legs
in the old roadrunner cartoons,
or like a space shot trying to connect earthlings with the moon
you try catching up with your dreams, fusing them together
here, with everything you are thinking, now,
but you are still, by a beat, behind time,

though inside time, too, & the language, like seasons
is always changing, is always out ahead of you
& you are what the music hears inside your dna rhythms;

language created every day by you, by someone else
& played out here, or anywhere else, for that matter,
in an improvised way, too, you are

the possibility of what you are listening to, now,
the music up in the rhythms—soukas, salsa, maracas—

words of a poem pulsating jazz notes toward the light

# MEMORY, AS A CIRCLE

because it is beyond midnight somewhere,
between total darkness & daybreak,
light, pure & simple
is an echo of someone hidden far back in memory,
an echo pulsating like a heartbeat, it has intensity,
like a drummer keeping time alive,
it follows the rhythms of an artist breathing
music through a face jumping from a canvas, extends itself
way up into a future you can't even see now but know
is there, perhaps a moon sliding slowly across
the geography of black skin that is sky, is like a notion
a pearl once evoked in the mind when it first saw it coming,
that it was a globe lit up like the round, gleaming eye of a panther,
or the idea of a black hole imploding with light,
was your smile, love, come here again, back from memory seducing,
a light pulsating through imitates your face, where you once were,
where all these years a hole shaped like a cut-out of you
flattened itself out daily against my longing

& eye see a fire burning way out there in the pitch
black desert of midnight,
perhaps it is a campfire encircled by lonely spirits back when
eye knew you as a deep-sea diving lover, always underwater,
entombed inside your own breath bubbling circles,
your silent voice now a chain-link of bubbles climbing forever upward,
toward the surface, light pure & simple,
an echo of itself, when the light was fading fast
the way out far above your memory, light still beyond a doorway,
perhaps through which a lost fish once swam looking for the way
back to that baited hook it once refused to bite on,
back when the promise of light above this language was clear,
reflective, was shimmering like great music, or poetry,
before night came back washing everything away in darknesss,

before they dredged up your once-shining face from that lake,
fish eaten, bloated beyond even faith,

our hope a memory now eye have held onto all this time,
beyond even what language is to great music,

beyond even what metaphor is to this poem

# SHADES OF BLUE FOR A BLUE BRIDGE

*for Mildred Howard, Joe Rudolph & Yori Wada*

1.

three shades of blue
evoke minnie's can do,
soo chow's, yori wada

2.

jimbo's bop city,
john lee's boom boom room,
history riffing blue matzoh balls,
fried chicken, soba

3.

the jigoku club inside
j town, bold rebels jamming
cross from black town, udon,
grits, barbecue

4.

cherry blossoms blooming
in lady day's hair, greens & fat back,
sashimi staining kimonos

5.

you walking filmore,
crossing geary with duke,
street cars running over ghost-tracks,
pigfeet in vinegar

6.

indigo-blue & white,
red satin, sticky fingers handling
chop sticks, hot cornbread,
sweet potato pie

7.

memories brought back
in a blue mirror, gefilte fish,
kimochi, lox & bagels

8.

filmore auditorium
jamming beneath miles of blue,
bird, monk, nihomachi.
a fake dividing line

9.

mixing it all up
this cultural jambalaya stew,
kabuki, white linen,
silk, coltrane

10.

music the glue singing
new images of multi-you
rapping in the sweet blue air

# TRANSCIRCULARITIES

across, beyond, moving toward the soon other coast,
transcending a change of appearance, as when
transfigurating a moment that is circular,
as the O of a dead man's mouth is a circle
sometimes after his last deep breath has been sucked in,
becomes the shape of a spinning snake chasing, or swallowing
its own tail, can be a sign, an omen, perhaps, of what has been
forgotten, erased from the circular thought-waves
history provides, the highway of metaphors:
bombs & bullets & flag-waving guiding the way into madness
drunk on power, the hypocrisy of slaughter bombastic
with language rooted in opposing religious fervors, greed,
the sad war dead made over into blood-dripping saints,
converted to propaganda-iconography,

now we find ourselves once again here, as yesterday,
our speech a copy of a copy of a copy,
our histories located in roots, clues underground, bleached
bones, skulls without vanity marking the spots where
ancestral voices once swelled & grew colorful as bright flowers
were there, rhythmic, beautiful, full of surprises, bold with the new
twists inside language grown fresh in an instant,
then suddenly gone, erased in a blink,
as history quickly removes those who lose wars of iconography,
even as music of their speech echoes choices they made
when they stood visible, unbroken, inside their own loved skins,
their heartbeats thumping drumbeats in time with their spirits,
their voices musical instruments, they sang & shaped
a language they danced to then, even now you still hear
echoes of its rhythms on our own tongues here

now the faces of those ghosts are invisible as death
coming in the dark, after midnight when most eyes shut down,
close themselves off to light, live only inside shifting dreams,

it is a roundabout way that we have brought ourselves here,
shrouded in this moment of looping shadows,
whispering in this graveyard of rundown tombstones,
whispering to the memory of what could have been, like autumn,
brown leaves scattered across asphalt, or dirt, or stone,
after the chill of coming winter's tongue sentenced them here
to the fate of dried corpses rotting on a battlefield,

the eyes of owls, their whooping language of mystery
our only companions here, as time tick-tocks down,
our eyes rotate upward toward where we think heaven is,
as if looking for a sign, hoping for a savior

# INDEX OF TITLES

## FUNDER ACKNOWLEDGMENTS

Coffee House Press is an independent nonprofit literary publisher. Our books are made possible through the generous support of grants and gifts from many foundations, corporate giving programs, individuals, and through state and federal support. This project received major funding from the National Endowment for the Arts, a federal agency. Coffee House Press also received support from the Minnesota State Arts Board, through an appropriation by the Minnesota State Legislature; and from grants from the Athwin Foundation; the Beim Foundation; Buuck Family Foundation; the Bush Foundation; the Butler Family Foundation; the Elmer and Eleanor Andersen Foundation; Lerner Family Foundation; the McKnight Foundation; the law firm of Schwegman, Lundberg, Woessner & Kluth, P.A.; St. Paul Companies; Target, Marshall Field's, and Mervyn's with support from the Target Foundation; James R. Thorpe Foundation; Wells Fargo Foundation Minnesota; West Group; the Woessner Freeman Foundation; and many individual donors.

To you and our many readers across the country,
we send our thanks for your continuing support.

*This activity is made possible in part by a grant from the Minnesota State Arts Board, through an appropriation by the Minnesota State Legislature and a grant from the National Endowment for the Arts.* MINNESOTA STATE ARTS BOARD

NATIONAL
ENDOWMENT
FOR THE ARTS